PRAISE FOR KIM O'DONNEL:

"I can't think of a more cordial or welcoming tone with which to invite possibly skeptical meat eaters into the world of delicious, accessible plant-based cooking. With her characteristic warmth and great sense of humor—and with no dogma—Kim O'Donnel presents a great set of compelling recipes that will draw everyone into a big, shared tent of healthier eating."

—MOLLIE KATZEN, AUTHOR OF *MOOSEWOOD COOKBOOK*

"Bravo Kim! I'm dubbing this book the International Meatless Monday cookbook. It taps so happily into the global zeitgeist for treading lightly on our planet. The recipes are pure pleasure, and not a fake meat product in sight. With so many tempting meals, who wouldn't ditch the butcher block for just one day a week?"

—DAVID JOACHIM, AUTHOR OF *THE FOOD SUBSTITUTIONS BIBLE AND MASTERING THE GRILL*

"It's a home cook-friendly project, both approachable and cautiously adventurous, with recipes like O'Donnel's meatless take on cassoulet (!) in which beans take center stage or her Maryland crab cake in which chickpeas stand in for the famous Chesapeake crustacean . . . O'Donnel makes the gradual shift to vegetarianism easy."

—*THE WASHINGTON CITY PAPER*

"A great primer for those transitioning to a meatless diet and looking to arm themselves with recipes for more substantial fare . . . A gentle reminder that small changes are great, too, and that we all need to make conscientious choices about our diet, for the planet and for our health."

—ECOCENTRIC.ORG

"An original concept that will help many carnivores help curb their habit."

—MIDWEST BOOK REVIEW

"An absolutely delicious addition to every eater's cookbook collection."

—FOODISTA BLOG

"Full of recipes for hearty and flavorful meals that give you the satisfying texture and complex layers of flavors that are missing from many vegetarian dishes that just omit the meat . . . [The] convivial tone makes it feel like Kim is in the kitchen with you, sharing her favorite tips and tricks."

—*SEATTLE WEEKLY'S* "COOKING THE BOOKS" BLOG

"This is an excellent book for people who are trying to eat less meat in their diet, especially those who may be having a hard time achieving that goal. It's also a wonderful book for people who are already vegetarian, with lots of variety."

—TREEHUGGER.COM

"This would make a great gift and perhaps a little nudge to those who would like to eat healthier without sacrificing a thing."

—*ECO MAMA'S GUIDE TO GREEN LIVING*

"Proof that there's no need to sacrifice taste on the altar of nutrition."

—*BOSTON HERALD*

"O'Donnel has a certain flair about her . . . These recipes are definitely worth trying."

—*SACRAMENTO BOOK REVIEW*

"Even though the meat is cut from the recipes, flavor is not sacrificed and that is what makes this cookbook so exceptional and highly recommended."

—*TUCSON CITIZEN*

"This book is ideal for those transitioning to a plant-based diet, though longtime vegetarians will surely find new inspiration, as well."

—PROJECTFOODIE.COM

"I only eat meat when it comes from animals that are responsibly raised, like we serve at Chipotle, otherwise, I find myself going meatless. In fact, I've significantly cut down on the amount of meat I eat. Kim O'Donnel's book is a great resource for people who love meat but also want to eat less of it."

—STEVE ELLS, FOUNDER, CHAIRMAN, AND CO-CEO, CHIPOTLE MEXICAN GRILL

"The landscape of childhood has changed—no longer are our children guaranteed a safe and healthy future—not in the face of climate change, obesity and heart disease. In *The Meat Lover's Meatless Cookbook*, Kim O'Donnel inspires us, using wit and wisdom, to recreate our families' carnivorous plates. With poignant reason, practical 'how to' advice, and a sensitivity to our culinary challenges and restrictions, *The Meat Lover's Meatless Cookbook* is an invaluable resource to anyone who eats."

—ROBYN O'BRIEN, MOTHER OF FOUR, FOUNDER, ALLERGYKIDS FOUNDATION

THE MEAT LOVER'S
MEATLESS
CELEBRATIONS

Year-Round Vegetarian Feasts
(You Can Really Sink Your Teeth Into)

KIM O'DONNEL

PHOTOGRAPHY BY CLARE BARBOZA

Da Capo
LIFE
LONG

A Member of the Perseus Books Group

Designed by Megan Jones Design (www.meganjonesdesign.com)
Set in 9 point DIN by Megan Jones Design (www.meganjonesdesign.com)

Cataloging-in-Publication data for this book is available from the Library of Congress.

First Da Capo Press edition 2012

ISBN: 978-0-7382-1594-5

Published by Da Capo Press
A Member of the Perseus Books Group
www.dacapopress.com

Note: The information in this book is true and complete to the best of our knowledge.
This book is intended only as an informative guide for those wishing to know more about
health issues. In no way is this book intended to replace, countermand, or conflict with
the advice given to you by your own physician. The ultimate decision concerning care
should be made between you and your doctor. We strongly recommend you follow his or
her advice. Information in this book is general and is offered with no guarantees on the
part of the authors or Da Capo Press. The authors and publisher disclaim all liability
in connection with the use of this book. The names and identifying details of people
associated with events described in this book have been changed. Any similarity to actual
persons is coincidental.

Da Capo Press books are available at special discounts for bulk purchases in the U.S. by
corporations, institutions, and other organizations. For more information, please contact
the Special Markets Department at the Perseus Books Group, 2300 Chestnut Street, Suite
200, Philadelphia, PA, 19103, or call (800) 810-4145, ext. 5000, or e-mail special.markets@
perseusbooks.com.

10 9 8 7 6 5 4 3 2 1

FOR MY PARENTS,

WHO TAUGHT ME HOW

TO COOK UP LIFE

contents

FALL

ELECTION NIGHT · 42

Spiced Nuts, Indian Style

Lentil "Meatballs" served with toothpicks, Swedish style, with Marinara Sauce for dipping

Stromboli

Tropical Fruit Plate with Chile-Lime Salt

Apple-Rosemary-Walnut Pie with Enlightened Pie Dough

Chocolate-Chile Pudding

THANKSGIVING · 43

Delicata Boats with Red Rice Stuffing

Roasted Red Onions with Pumpkin-Rosemary Stuffing and Root Vegetable Gravy

Maple Crans

Sweet Potato–Pesto Gratin

Hot Brussels Sprouts Slaw

Apple-Rosemary-Walnut Pie with Enlightened Pie Dough

Pumpkin Pudding

Molasses Cookies

WINTER

WARMING UP TO WINTER WINGDING · 62

Potato-Turnip Gratin with Blue Cheese Sauce

Carrot-Fennel Soup

Broiled Grapefruit Rounds with Massaged Frisée Salad

Cranberry-Pistachio Biscotti

Chocolate Bark

HANUKKAH: HOT OIL TREATMENT · 72

Family-Style Latke

Horseradish Yogurt "Cream"

Applesauce

Spinach Pakoras

Hush Puppies

Chickpea Fries

Chocolate Bark

SPRING

PASSOVER · 136

Arugula Matzo Lasagna

Roasted Asparagus with Gremolata and Almond Star Dust

Dessert option: Quinoa-Walnut Brownies

SPRING BREAK PATTY PARTY · 139

Greek Patty

Feta-Yogurt Sauce

Jamaican Patty

Pineapple Salsa

Southern-Fried Chick . . . Pea

Caramelized Onions

Finger-Licking Barbecue Sauce

Jicama Salad

Rhubarb Buckle

Fro-Yo Affogato

SALUTING MOM AND DAD · 150

HERS

Chickpea Crepes with Zesty Mashed Potatoes and Indian-Spiced Spinach Sauce

Roasted Asparagus with Gremolata and Almond Star Dust

Rhubarb-Strawberry Fool

HIS

Chickpea Fries with Finger-Licking Barbecue Sauce

Double Black Bean Burgers

Caesar-y Romaine Salad with Roasted Tofu "Croutons"

Blueberry Buckle

CINCO DE MAYO · 166

Sandra's Sopes

Sofrito-Seasoned Black Beans

Pico de Gallo

Strawberry and Pepita Salad

Chocolate-Chile Pudding

SUMMER

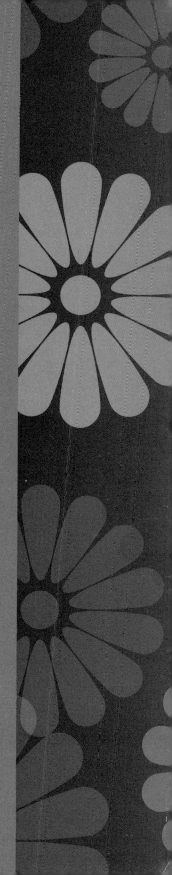

LAUGHTER IS

BRIGHEST WHERE

THE FOOD IS

—IRISH PROVERB

INTRODUCTION

Thanksgiving, 2005. My pals Liz and Matt invited me to Matt's parents' house for the big meal. As my contribution, I made a tofu pumpkin pie, a decision that brought smiles to the newly vegetarian couple but elicited nervous laughter from the hosts. A pie filled with soybean curd was not on the table in Norman Rockwell's famous Thanksgiving painting. But my pie was hardly a shock compared to what was to precede it on the table. Liz and Matt had requested real estate on Mom and Dad's turkey-centric table for a boxed Tofurky roast with all the trimmings. The meatless fixin's were innocuous enough: a drab monochromatic scheme of gray (or was it beige?) that reminded me of hospital bed fare, a striking example of "meatless at any cost," especially taste. I had one bite of that faux turkey, which was more than enough.

The symbolism of the curd bird and pie ran deep. Our additions to the holiday table were perceived as odd, even otherworldly (and certainly not festive), setting the stage for an us-versus-them dynamic. Frankly, the real bird wasn't doing much for me, either, but our menu additions were challenging the Rockwell status quo, the way things had always been done. It's as if Liz and Matt ripped open the dining room ceiling and ushered in a lightning storm.

Um, please pass the rolls. . . .

If you're too young to remember Rockwell, surely you understand the feeling from *How the Grinch Stole Christmas!* the infinitely charming Dr. Seuss tale of a villain and his efforts to squelch the holidays for the townsfolk of Who-ville, which includes absconding with the "roast beast." Those two words are how the kids of my generation came to refer to the meaty centerpiece of any holiday feast: ham or lamb for Easter, spare ribs, franks and burgers on the Fourth of July, corned beef and cabbage for Saint Patrick's Day, andouille gumbo for Mardi Gras, and of course, turkey on Thanksgiving. A feast without the beast was unheard of.

Living out one's dietary dreams, à la Liz and Matt, was best done in the privacy of one's own kitchen. Out of the home, and particularly at family gatherings, the meatless way of eating simply got in the way.

How quickly things have changed.

In 2008, as part of an effort to take charge of my health and lighten my carbon footprint, I lessened my lifelong grip on the bone and got my meat-loving husband to join me on a Meatless Monday–style adventure. Rather than completely break up with meat, we took one day off, incremental baby-step bites that helped us create a new normal—and led to the collection of recipes in *The Meat Lover's Meatless Cookbook*.

When we first got going, I promised him "delicious first, meatless second," a standard that has stood the test of time. Fast-forward four years: What started out as an experiment has become our preferred way of eating. Our plant-based suppers now outweigh the meaty ones not only because they're nutritionally virtuous but because they're downright delicious. They've tapped us into a world of cuisines, flavors, and textures that previously we had only read about. Along the eat-less-meat way, we discovered both the necessity and joys of umami, a phenomenon commonly associated with bacon and other meaty morsels. Roughly translated as "savoriness," this Japanese term is referred to as the fifth flavor, along with sweet, sour, bitter, and salty. The best way I can describe it is the mouth-coating phenomenon and lingering finish of certain ingredients that make us smack our lips and say, "Wow, that's delicious." Much to our delight, we discovered that the plant world is loaded with umami-rich ingredients, including molasses, mushrooms, mustard, roasted vegetables, smoked paprika, and soy sauce (see page 18).

Still, when it was time to entertain and put on a spread of grander proportions for friends and family, I would fall back into my "roast beast" comfort zone, as if nothing had changed. If we were able to rock out the meatless umami for our everyday meals, I wondered why I was stumbling as a hostess with the meatless mostest.

It turns out that I'm not alone. About one-third of meat-loving Americans are embarking on similar eat-less-meat journeys, many referring to themselves as "flexitarian." And as we redefine who we are by what we eat, the dietary divide is blurring. Gone are the days when vegetarians like Liz and Matt are the weird outcasts at family gatherings; now Thanksgiving and the calendar's myriad celebratory feasts are truly mixed-diet

affairs catering to eaters of all dietary stripes. And speaking of affairs, we're falling into mixed-diet relationships at seemingly unprecedented rates, resulting in dynamics perhaps never seen before at the table. I'm sure you've met Valerie the vegan who's fallen in love with your brother, Mister I-can't-live-without-my-sausages. Your neighbors Mom and Pop Omnivore are reeling from the news that their teenaged son Burger Boy is now swearing off "anything with a face." And remember your best friend's lacto-ovo cousin who always brings the best-ever stuffing? She's just been diagnosed with a gluten intolerance. Sound familiar?

The new challenge, then, is in figuring out how to meet at the table (without meat on the table) not only at the end of the day but on all of the special days, when we want to yip it up.

My quest for a "feast without the beast" put me back in the kitchen, where I've cooked up more than two dozen ways to eat and be merry for all kinds of occasions. You won't find faux turkey or simulated hot dogs here but seasonal produce, legumes, whole grains—and plenty of "delicious first."

We ring in the New Year with good-luck black-eyed peas in paella form. As your guide, I'll lead the way through the calendar of holidays, making stops for lentil "meatball" subs for the football playoffs, Cajun blackened tofu for Mardi Gras, and grilled zucchini heroes on the Fourth of July. We'll fete Mom and Dad, with chickpea crepes, double black bean burgers, and rhubarb-strawberry fool.

I've got Thanksgiving—the mac daddy of gastronomic holidays—covered, too: a sumptuous spread that includes delicata squash boats with red rice stuffing, sweet potato–kale pesto gratin, Brussels sprouts slaw, and, of course, good ole American apple pie, but with an enlightened butter–olive oil dough.

Scattered in between are the sundry milestones marked on our personal calendars—birthdays, anniversaries, engagements, graduations, promotions, league championships—the many other happy occasions that make us wanna hoot, holler, and cook up a storm.

Last but definitely not least, you'll get a peek into a relatively new but rapidly expanding part of my kitchen life—food preservation. My only regret about canning is that I waited so long. Learning how to extend the season of my favorite fruits and vegetables in a jar is one of the most gratifying and useful skills I've acquired as an adult. In addition to the basics of water-bath canning (plus some tricks I've learned since founding Canning Across America in 2009), I share a few of my favorite preserved and pickled recipes to help get you started.

There is so much good food in this new collection, I can hardly sit still. Once again, I invite you to join me and the motley crew of dining companions that we've become as we celebrate, all together, the deliciousness of plants and the joys of gathering at the table.

HOW TO USE THIS BOOK

There are a total of twenty-six menus on the pages that follow. While some menus are extensive, others are more of a tip of the hat, with stories and ideas on how to build your own feast. Covering all four seasons, they salute a mix of federally observed secular holidays (when you might have the day off); some of the major Judeo-Christian holidays; cultural and ethnic days of commemoration; and the many festivities in our personal date books, from anniversaries to reunions.

I've also created four seasonally themed menus designed as catchalls for holidays and cultural observances that fall close to each other on the calendar. Consider the Warming Up to Winter Wingding menu during the jam-packed month of December, or the Spring Forward Feast as the calendar approaches Easter, Earth Day, and Mother's Day.

With a few exceptions, the menus are designed to serve a party of six (with plenty of leftovers if it's just four of you) with a minimum of four dishes, including dessert. Ambitious go-getters will prepare the entire menu, but that's hardly necessary. There's no pressure, just lots of options to mix and match and come up with your own interpretation of a celebratory repast.

In some instances, I share a centerpiece dish that is more time intensive and has several steps or moving parts. The Eggplant Timpano, Black-Eyed

Pea Paella, and Potato-Turnip Gratin with Blue Cheese Sauce all come to mind. They are meals unto themselves, but have been paired with simple sides if you really want to gild the lily. Some menus will feel like a casual buffet, such as the pan-Asian options for Lunar New Year or the mix of *chaat*-style small plates for Diwali. Other menus, such as Thanksgiving and New Year's, will feel more like a banquet. In some cases, I cull dishes from throughout the collection around a certain theme. Although latkes are front and center on the Hanukkah menu, I've dished up other suggestions for the ultimate fry fest that would be fun at any time of the year. For Halloween, it's all things orange, a beta-carotene-rich antidote to the trick-or-treat loot.

In many other menus, the recipes work together as an ensemble cast. Leave one dish out, and the show will still go on deliciously. Within these ensemble-style menus are dishes that come together in an hour and can easily be "dressed down" for weeknight suppers. I've curated the most weeknight-friendly dishes into a seven-day planner that can be sliced and diced however you wish. To lighten the day-to-day load, I've got make-ahead tips and suggested dishes to prep on the weekend and enjoy into the week.

A note on the desserts: I like a sweet ending—but not too sweet or fussy. I'm a sucker for the homespun comfort and ease of American classics—such treats as fruit crisp, buckle, and pie. With "delicious first" as the priority, I set out to include some kind of healthful twist to the dessert offerings. Wherever I could, I dialed back the amount of sugar, dairy fat, and eggs, without compromising flavor or texture. Instead of a whipped cream topping, I froth up Greek yogurt, and my pie dough has an unorthodox blend of butter and olive oil. This mission also helped pave the way for a small handful of vegan desserts, some of which are also gluten free.

In the top corner of each recipe, you'll notice graphic icons that let you know if something is gluten-free, dairy- and egg-free (a.k.a. vegan), as well as dairy-optional. Although the menus have families in mind, I've called out dishes that particularly resonated with kids during recipe testing. Here's the key:

DO = dairy optional
GF = gluten-free
KIDDO = kid-friendly
V = vegan, also known as dairy- and egg-free

You may notice that pantry staples—butter, eggs, oil, onions, salt—are listed in the recipes without specifics on size or type (*Does she mean a medium egg or jumbo?*). Here's what I mean when I say:

BUTTER: unsalted
EGGS: large
NEUTRAL OIL: grapeseed, rice bran, safflower
ONIONS: yellow
SALT: fine sea salt

You'll find deeper explanation on these and many other staples in *The Meat Lover's Meatless Pantry* (page 7), a fully stocked glossary of the

ingredients featured on these pages. Many of the ingredients will be familiar and readily available at your local food shopping destinations, from big-box stores to ethnic markets. That said, readers in more remote areas generally have to work harder to source supplies. (I recall one intrepid recipe tester in rural Kentucky who had to travel a few hours to find bittersweet chocolate.) I've compiled my go-to list of online vendors and suppliers to eliminate those worries no matter where you live. Even the Chinese fermented black beans (probably the least familiar ingredient to my recipe testers) are readily available in Asian grocery stores and online. I've also shared some of my favorite Web destinations, where I get informed and enlightened.

Last but certainly not least, I'd like to share a few all-purpose suggestions as you navigate through the book and your life in the kitchen:

- Read through the entire recipe (and in some cases, the entire menu) at least twice before you fire up the stove and sharpen the knives. It may sound daft, but the more we get in the habit of reading the kitchen road map and visualizing the twists and turns of a recipe, the more aware and mindful we become as cooks.

- Know your oven and stovetop. I developed and tested all the recipes using a gas oven and four-burner stovetop. Some of my testers worked with electric stoves and coiled stovetops, others with ceramic or glass flat tops. Cooking times may vary, and you are the best judge in that department. To keep an eye on whether the internal temperature of the oven matches the number I've punched on the keypad, I use a hanging oven thermometer. Although not foolproof (they periodically need to be replaced), the oven thermometer is helpful in sussing out hotspots.

- I won't get into the business of telling you how to outfit your kitchen, with the exception of two items: a sharp knife and a salad spinner. A sharp knife slides through onions and doesn't bruise herbs. It makes chopping breezy fun, not sluggish tedium. Don't know how or don't care to learn? Take it to your local hardware or cookware store to find out who in your area puts the edge back in a blade. Many farmers' markets are now offering knife-sharpening services as well. Get this done on a quarterly basis. The best way to maintain that edge for as long as possible is to use a honing (or sharpening) steel. (It's that rodlike object with a handle that may be collecting dust in your kitchen drawer.) Hone your knife every time you plan to use it: Hold the knife in your dominant hand and the steel in the other hand. Place the heel (the bottom end) of the knife perpendicular to the steel at about a 30-degree angle. Move the blade from heel to tip along the steel, repeating about ten times per side.

- The other Very Important Item is a salad spinner. Life won't end without one, but it will be so much crisper and more satisfying. Dry, crisp greens and herbs can be the difference between enjoying vegetables and eating them under duress. They are *that* much better after a few turns in the salad spinner.

· Have fun. Cooking is an opportunity to step away from the worries of the day and focus on the creation of something that stimulates all five physical senses. The snap of a bean, the hiss of a hot skillet, the perfume of a pie, the crunch of a carrot. In the documentary *How to Cook Your Life*, Zen priest and cookbook author Edward Espe Brown says, "With cooking, your hands get to be hands. They get to actually do something [rather] than sitting around entertaining yourself with your iPod and your Internet. Our hands don't get to do much anymore."

So if we follow his advice and let our hands be hands, and we chop and stir and bang around the kitchen to make a meal with the people we love the most, we are, one crumb at a time, taking charge of our health and our lives. Here's to keeping the spirit of cooking alive!

THE MEAT LOVER'S MEATLESS PANTRY

ALLSPICE: Also known as pimento and Jamaica pepper, allspice is a berry of an evergreen tree native to the West Indies and South America. Dark brown when dried, it resembles the black peppercorn but is bigger and more cylindrical. Its flavor is both pungent and peppery, an argument for modest use. The molasses cookies on page 60 wouldn't be the same without it.

AROMATICS: This refers to any combination of onions, celery, carrots, sweet or chile peppers, garlic, and ginger, often the foundation of curries, sauces, soups, and stews.

BEANS: Dried or canned? There are reasons for having both on hand. Personally, I prefer the texture and flavor of dried beans, but they do require several hours of soaking (and there's something to be said for the convenience of opening a can of beans). Some canned beans perform better than others; in my experience, black beans, chickpeas, and red kidney beans, generally speaking, are among the sturdiest varieties. The flipside: Many brands of canned beans are high in sodium, so keep an eye out for low- or no-sodium offerings. And there's the BPA issue. BPA is bisphenol-A, a chemical that is used in the manufacturing of canned goods and it remains at the center of a controversy over potential associated health risks. Eden Foods remains the only company I know of that uses BPA-free cans. For every bean recipe in this collection, I tested with both canned and dried beans and share my recommendations for the best performer.

BLACK BEANS, FERMENTED: Also sold as salted black beans, these are black soybeans that have been preserved in salt and are a staple of the Chinese pantry. They are pungent and complex in flavor. Look for them in Asian markets in vacuum-sealed bags or cans. To soften, soak in equal parts water before using, and store in a jar in a dark place, where they'll keep indefinitely.

BLACK BEANS, TURTLE: These are the beans commonly associated with the burritos, chili, and nachos of Tex-Mex cookery. They have an earthy flavor, creamy texture and play nice with a variety of flavors. They will be part of my last supper.

BLACK-EYED PEAS: Also known as cowpeas, these little off-white legumes are native to Africa. Their "black eye" is more of a yin-yang swirl on their side. In the American South, they're considered a harbinger of good luck if eaten on New Year's Day.

BLANCHING: To partially cook by boiling for a short time, followed by a quick plunge in ice-cold water to halt the cooking. A useful technique that helps mellow out bitter greens, set the color of herbs and green vegetables, ease tough skins off fruit, and jumpstart long-cooking vegetables.

BLOOD ORANGE: A variety of orange that always wins the beauty pageant with its scarlet ruby (or is it garnet?) flesh that tastes like it collided into a patch of raspberries. It's a heaven-sent combination of sweet and tart that sparkles on the tongue. Look for it in the supermarket produce section between December and March.

BOK CHOY: A member of the very large and extensive Brassica vegetable family. *Bok choy* refers to several types of leafy greens with white or green stalks in various sizes. I am partial to the tender-leafed, dwarflike bunches of baby bok choy available in Asian markets and specialty markets, and at farmers' markets when in season (spring and fall). The full-size bunches are more readily available in supermarket produce sections.

BROCCOLI RABE: Also known as rapini and raab, broccoli rabe looks like skinny broccoli, but it is more closely related to the turnip. Its flowering stem and leaves have a slightly bitter flavor that calls for blanching before sautéing. Loves teaming up with garlic, as demonstrated in the Big Game menu (page 91).

BRUSSELS SPROUTS: Often maligned and misunderstood, these mini cabbages are savory morsels when roasted rather than boiled or slivered into a hot slaw (page 54). A cold-weather darling at farmers' markets.

BUTTER: Unsalted. Salted butter is great at the table, but it's a wild card at the stove. Salt content varies from brand to brand, so it's hard to know just how much salt you're adding to a dish. You have more control adding salt on its own. Unless I'm baking, I use butter infrequently, so I keep it in the freezer. Look for brands that state on the label that the milk is organic or from cows not treated with the artificial growth hormone rBST (also known as rBGH).

CARDAMOM: It's difficult to describe the flavor and aroma of the blackish-brown seeds extracted from their green husklike pods. Kind of peppery, yet pungent like cloves, with a little citrus thrown in, cardamom adds layers of enigmatic flavor (and perfume) in only a way that cardamom can do. The essential oils are volatile and have a short life span, so buy from a trusted spice source (see Resources) or in the bulk spice area of your supermarket where turnover will be higher than in the packaged jars on the shelves.

CHARD: Short for Swiss chard, a quick-cooking leafy green from the beet family. Available during cool months, with a variety of gorgeous, almost neon-colored stalks and can be used interchangeably with spinach.

CHICKPEAS: Resist the temptation to be non-plussed by their uninspiring shade of beige; chickpeas are nutty, buttery, and perhaps the meatiest legume of all. Because of their sturdy composition and versatile personality, I've been able to create the Spring Break Patty Party menu (page 139), a trio of chickpea-based burgers with different culturally based flavor profiles. No other bean is as open, playful, and simply marvelous. Also known as *ceci*, *channa*, and garbanzo beans.

CHICKPEA FLOUR: Also known as garbanzo and gram flour. Mild in flavor rather than beany, it is good natured (albeit slightly clumpy), and plays nicely with a variety of flavors. In this collection, it assumes many roles, including "fries," (page 159), crepes (page 153), and as the crispy coating for *pakoras* (page 34), Indian fritters. Available in Indian markets and natural foods markets. A part of the Bob's Red Mill product line.

CHILE PEPPERS: I use both dried and fresh chile peppers with various flavor profiles and levels of heat.

Dried and ground: I'm partial to cayenne, chipotle, New Mexico, and paprika, both hot and smoked.

Fresh: I'm a fool for the fruitiness of the habanero but realize that not everyone appreciates its blazing heat. Similarly, I love the Scotch bonnet, but they are more difficult to source. I like the jalapeño for its moderate heat, thick flesh, and supermarket availability (and especially love them pickled—see recipe on page 210), but the flavor tends to be grassy. For more punch, I prefer the equally available serrano.

CHIPOTLE CHILE PEPPER POWDER: The ground version of smoked jalapeño chiles. The flavor is both fiery and smoky, and is a good, although spicier, substitute for smoked paprika. A workhorse spice in my kitchen.

COCONUT MILK: These days, I keep two kinds of coconut milk on hand—canned and cartoned. Until recently, unsweetened coconut milk imported from Vietnam and Thailand was available only in cans. With its signature rich flavor and creamy texture, it's indispensable for curries, soups, and sauces. Then I found out about fortified coconut milk, a new product available in refrigerated and shelf-stable cartons in natural foods and specialty markets. With a thinner consistency similar to cow's milk and a nearly undetectable coconut flavor, coconut milk 2.0 is really versatile and shows great promise as the next dairy-free darling. I use the unsweetened version of So Delicious brand for many of the dairy-free desserts in these pages, as well as for the Hush Puppies (page 99).

COLLARD GREENS: If you look at the striated lily pad leaves of collards, you can tell they're related to cabbage. But they certainly eat more like their leafy cousin kale than like their bobbly-headed relative the Brussels sprout. As hearty cold-weather greens, they show up at farmers' markets all winter long. Despite the lore, collards don't need to be stewed in bacon fat to be loveable. Exhibit A: Thai curried collards (page 107).

CORIANDER: A plant that delivers a twofer—the feathery green leaves, also known as the herb cilantro—and the dried yellow-brown seeds, which are used as a spice. They taste nothing alike; the seeds are both bright and subtle in flavor, a mix of citrus, mustard, and maybe even sage. The leaves are harder to describe, musky yet lemon/lime-y and for some, downright soapy.

CUMIN: Available in both seed and ground form. The small pointy seeds (which resemble caraway seeds) impart terrific flavor when toasted. Used in Middle Eastern, Mexican, and Caribbean cookery, cumin has a musky smell and warm feel on the tongue.

DELICATA SQUASH: An oblong, thin-skinned variety of winter squash with a creamy gold flesh that is reminiscent of corn and sweet potatoes. This is a personal favorite, and wait 'til you see it stuffed with red rice for Thanksgiving (page 45).

EGGS: Large; that's the size I used for testing all of the recipes. As for the deciding factors in purchasing, my priorities are the hens' diet and how much room they have to roam. First choice: the neighborhood farmers' market or farm stands (or if I'm lucky, from a friend with a backyard coop!). The egg seller will be able to tell you what the hens eat and describe their living quarters, which should be lots of open pasture. Second choice: a supermarket that sells organic, pastured eggs from a local or regional source. On the carton, look for the word *pastured* rather than *cage-free*; the latter could still mean crowded living quarters.

FENNEL: Native to Italy, fennel has a celery-like bulb and dill-like fronds. Its flavor is delicately sweet and licorice-like but more herbal. Can be roasted, braised, thrown into soups (page 66), or sliced thinly and added to salads.

FENNEL SEED: The seeds of the nonbulbing variety of fennel that, when toasted, have an earthy, umami-rich flavor.

FRISÉE: A member of the chicory family that includes radicchio, escarole, and Belgian endive. Its curly, bitter leaves need taming with a citrus vinaigrette and some fine chopping, or you run the risk of eating something akin to hay. Once tamed, it is a festive-looking winter green and a great foil to fat. You'll see it in all its glory in the Warming Up to Winter menu (page 62).

GARLIC SCAPES: The curlicue green shoot of a developing garlic bulb. Tender like a scallion, with a mild garlic flavor. Makes amazing pesto (page 189). Because the scape represents a specific stage in the life of the garlic plant, it is available for a limited time in early summer.

GINGER, FRESH: Although it's often called gingerroot, this tropical plant is actually a rhizome, related to turmeric and cardamom. Its khaki-colored skin is easily peeled away with a teaspoon, and it can be sliced, grated, and mashed in a mortar and pestle. It makes frequent appearances in this collection.

GINGER, CRYSTALLIZED: Also known as candied ginger, fresh ginger is cooked in a syrup, then coated with sugar. Keeps indefinitely in the freezer.

GRANULATED SUGAR: Unless I have specified otherwise in the recipe, I'm referring to a less refined, unbleached sugar—but one that still pours and bakes like the white stuff we all grew up on. Among the countless options now in the marketplace, I turn to Florida Crystals, which is readily available in conventional supermarkets and big-box retailers as well as specialty and natural foods stores. The company also manufactures the more granular Demerara sugar (also known as raw sugar), which I like to use when I'm looking for a coarser texture (e.g., when topping the molasses cookies, page 60).

GREEK YOGURT: The latest craze to hit the dairy section, Greek yogurt is a thicker, creamier variation of plain yogurt that has been drained of its liquid whey. With an appealing umami-like mouthfeel, it is a terrific stand-in for sour cream and even whipped cream. The many supermarket brands to choose from include Chobani, Fage, and The Greek Gods.

JICAMA: Often ignored in the produce section, jicama is a big bulbous root vegetable that is surprisingly thin-skinned and easy to cut. Crunchy like an apple yet mild like a water chestnut, it is a refreshing option for salads and crudités platters. It's also seriously low-cal—just 50 calories per cup.

JERK SAUCE: A highly aromatic and flavorful marinade and barbecue sauce from Jamaica. The commercial brands I've used with success include Busha Browne's Spicy Jerk Sauce, Walkerswood Jerk Barbecue Sauce and Dave's Gourmet Jammin' Jerk Sauce & Marinade. Look in the condiments section of your supermarket or online. Try to avoid brands using high-fructose corn syrup.

KALE: A member of the cabbage family, kale is an all-purpose, leafy cool-weather green loaded with nutrients. It is one of my favorite, go-to leafy greens. Lacinato (a.k.a. dinosaur) kale is at the top of my list, where it's featured in the addictive Raw Kale Salad (page 119).

LEMONGRASS: This aromatic herb grows into a tall stalk with raspy tips and a bulb at its base. An essential ingredient in Thai and Vietnamese pantries. Available in Asian markets and in specialty markets. Grows well in hot climates.

LENTILS: One of the first known domesticated crops, with links to the fertile crescent of the Stone Age, the lentil is as ancient as food gets. Revered in nearly every corner of the world, the lentil is finally catching on in the United States, where its quick-cooking (no soaking required), versatile personality is attracting attention. In these pages, I use the ubiquitous brown lentil and the smaller Spanish Pardina (which is also brown).

MASA HARINA: Dried corn kernels are soaked and cooked in limewater, a process called nixtamalization. The resulting masa ("dough" in Spanish) is then milled into the powdery flour known as masa harina. It is the foundation of corn tortillas and many traditional dishes of Mexican and Central American cookery, including arepas and *sopes* (page 167). The most readily available brand is Maseca; the lone non-GMO brand I know of is Bob's Red Mill.

MOLASSES, BLACKSTRAP: The residual product of sugarcane production. Blackstrap molasses is the result of the third boiling of sugarcane syrup and it's unmistakably dark, thick, and more pungent than sweet. Look for unsulfured varieties, which are processed without sulfur dioxide. Wholesome Sweeteners is a certified organic and Fair Trade brand. It's surprisingly rich in umami and is a secret ingredient in the Caesar-y Salad (page 162).

OIL, FLAVORED: Oils with a distinctive flavor, not artificially flavored. The two most frequently used flavored oils in my kitchen are olive oil and sesame oil. The distinctive fruitiness of olive oil clashes with Asian and Indian spice-intensive dishes in the book, and its lower smoking point creates a challenge for longer cook times. On the other hand, this oil is tailor-made for vinaigrettes and pestos, or for drizzling over pasta or vegetables just before serving. For uncooked applications, feel free to use unfiltered small-batch extra-virgin oil so you can really appreciate the nuances in flavor. For use at the stove in small amounts, I like Spectrum, Colavita, and 365, the private label at Whole Foods Market.

As for sesame oil, I prefer the darker, richer flavor of the toasted variety. I use as a flavor enhancer rather than a cooking medium, as too much can be overwhelming and burn quickly. If you decide to cook with it, add a neutral oil to increase its smoking point.

OIL, NEUTRAL: For sautéing, frying, stir-frying, and other high-heat methods, I prefer to use flavorless, all-purpose oils. Over the past few years, I've become a fan of rice bran oil, which has a very high smoking point (485°F) and midpoint price tag. However, it's less accessible than safflower or grapeseed oil, my second and third choices. (See Resources on page 216 for where to find it.) Now that Spectrum produces organic canola oil, I've added it to the list. (The majority of canola oil is made from genetically engineered seed; read the non-GMO entry for background.)

ONION: Unless specified, I'm referring to the yellow onion (also known as a yellow storage onion), an all-purpose year-round allium with a good balance of sweetness and pungency.

PARCHMENT PAPER: A silicone-treated paper with nonstick and high-heat capabilities. Lining baking sheets and pans is just one of its many functions; I use it as a cover, wrapper, pastry surface, storage liner, and on a rare occasion, party hat. It's an essential tool in my kitchen. Look for unbleached brown paper; Beyond Gourmet is a commercially available brand.

PARMIGIANO-REGGIANO: Many of us grew up with the tall green can of shelf-stable "Parmesan" that we dutifully sprinkled atop spaghetti and meatballs. Now we've got a taste of the real thing—hard, aged cow's milk cheese from the Emilia-Romagna region of Italy. Parm-Regg virgins may balk at the price tag, but I promise you: A little goes a long way,

and when stored in cheese paper (see Resources), it keeps for a few months.

PARSNIP: That white, carrot-looking thing in the produce section is a parsnip, a versatile and highly underrated root vegetable. Faintly sweet with hints of parsley flavor and a creamy texture. The star of the Root Vegetable Gravy (page 46).

PARSLEY, FRESH: I prefer flat-leaf over curly, but I won't let curly hold up a recipe if that's what is available. Chopped, you can hardly tell which is which; whole, they are different in both appearance and texture.

PEARL BARLEY: A form of this ancient grain that has been "pearled" (polished and steamed) to remove both the bran and outer husk. As a result, it is considered a refined rather than whole grain and cooks more quickly than its less processed counterparts. Still, pearl barley is a respectable source of fiber; ½ cup of cooked pearl barley contains 3 grams of dietary fiber.

PECORINO: A hard, grateable Italian cheese made from sheep's milk and a great alternative to Parmigiano-Reggiano, for those who are allergic to cow's milk.

PEPITAS: Also known as hulled pumpkin seeds, olive-shaded pepitas add richness and texture, and when toasted, become nutty. Available in the bulk areas in some supermarkets and in Latino markets.

POMEGRANATE MOLASSES: Actually, this acts a lot more like a syrup than the molasses we know made from sugar cane. Pomegranate juice is boiled and reduced into a gorgeous shade of red wine; on the lips, it's sweet, tart, and pungent in an umami-rich way. Available in Middle East or Mediterranean markets.

POTATOES: For the handful of dishes in the collection that feature potatoes, I favor thin-skinned medium-starch varieties such as Yellow Finn and Yukon Gold, which are great mashed and in gratins. My third choice is the good ole reliable russet, also known as the Idaho potato.

QUINOA: This supernutritious, delicious, and versatile seed of an ancient plant from the goosefoot family (beets, chard, spinach) acts like a grain. Native to the Andean regions of South America, it is a complete protein, cooks as easily as rice, and is a terrific gluten-free stand-in. Available in shades of beige, red, black, and a multicolored "rainbow" mix. Easily grinds into flour, which is featured in the brownies (page 97) and jam-dot cookies (page 132).

RICE, BHUTANESE RED: A medium-grain heirloom variety native to the Himalayas, with a nutty, slightly sweet flavor, and chewy texture. The American–born and bred Wehani, developed from basmati seeds, is a very good long-grain stand-in. Available in specialty markets and in the bulk areas of natural food markets, as well as online.

RICE, BROWN: Before white rice is milled and polished, it's brown rice, with its fiber-rich bran and germ intact. Unlike white rice, brown rice is a whole grain with a distinctively nutty flavor and toothsome texture. Long-, medium-, or short-grain, it's become the go-to rice at our house.

RICE, SHORT-GRAIN WHITE: In these pages, used for the risotto filling of the eggplant *timpano* (page 23) and the black-eyed pea paella (page 78). When stirred in liquid over time, it releases a lusciously creamy starch. Varieties to look for include Arborio, Carnaroli, and Vialone Nano, which are available in specialty markets.

RICE FLOUR: Fine-grained powdery flour made from white rice. Not to be confused with sweet rice flour. Available in Asian markets and in specialty markets. Part of the Bob's Red Mill product line.

SAFFRON: It's infamously expensive but these hand-harvested stigmas of the crocus flower are worth experiencing in the kitchen. The flavor is slightly bitter, the aroma both delicate and pungent. Saffron appears in the paella (page 78) and the Indian-spiced poached pears (page 40).

SALT: Salt from evaporated seawater is what I'm using (see some notes on page 18 for my thoughts on kosher salt). I used fine sea salt in testing the recipes, and buy brands that indicate place of origin on the label. When I'm looking for texture and a pop of minerality on a finished dish, I use

Maldon flakes or sel gris, a versatile mineral-rich gray salt also known as Celtic sea salt. Fine sea salt and Maldon flakes are available in specialty supermarkets and some conventional supermarkets. Regardless of brand, look for these buzz words: *unrefined*, *unbleached*, *trace minerals*. Look for sel gris and other gourmet salts through The Meadow, author and salt expert Mark Bitterman's salt emporium. (See Resources for details.)

SHALLOT: A member of the allium family, the shallot looks like garlic (bulbs, thin skin) but cuts like a red onion, and is more delicate and sweeter than a storage onion.

SHAOXING RICE WINE: A type of rice wine from China, Shaoxing is amber in color and similar in flavor to dry sherry (but not cooking sherry). Your best bet for tracking it down is an Asian market or online source.

SMOKED PAPRIKA: Also known as *pimentón de la vera* in Spain, smoked paprika is made from peppers that have been slowly smoked, resulting in a sublime mixture of heat, sweet, and smoke. This is among my most beloved spices. Increasingly available in conventional supermarkets and through online spice resources.

SPLIT PEAS: These little pale green disks are a variety of field peas grown specifically for drying. As they dry, they naturally split. Like lentils, they require no soaking and cook in about forty minutes.

SWEET POTATOES: There are two commercially available varieties: one with a yellowish skin and with a pale yellow flesh, the other with a darker, thicker skin and a deep orange flesh. I prefer the latter and used it to create the recipes. Some people confuse this deep orange sweet potato with garnet yams and often refer to them as such. They are actually unrelated, despite the resemblance.

SRIRACHA: The general name for a hot sauce from Thailand, but also the namesake brand made by Huy Fong in California. Known for its fiery pungent flavor, the red jalapeño chile sauce, packaged in its signature clear plastic bottle with the rooster logo, has developed a cult following.

TAHINI: Made from ground sesame seeds, tahini has the look and feel of creamy peanut butter. It is a staple of Middle East cuisine. Once opened, keep refrigerated, as the oils will eventually oxidize and go rancid. Available in many supermarkets, specialty markets, and Middle East markets.

TAPIOCA, QUICK-COOKING: This is the granulated form of this starch made from the cassava plant, used to thicken cherry and berry pie fillings. Not to be confused with pearl tapioca.

THAI RED CURRY PASTE: A pounded mixture of herbs, spices, and chile peppers, this paste is ready made and available in conventional supermarkets and Asian markets. You'll see it packaged in either a can or small glass jar. Leftover paste can be stored in an airtight container in the refrigerator.

TOFU: Made from soybean curd, tofu comes in a variety of textures. For the savory recipes in this collection, you'll work with either extra-firm or firm tofu, which is packed in water and found in the refrigerated section of the supermarket. For the desserts, you'll use silken tofu, which is packed in shelf-stable boxes often found on supermarket shelves with Asian ingredients. My go-to nationally available brands for fresh tofu are Nasoya, Wildwood, and Woodstock Farms. For silken tofu, I look for Mori-Nu, which is readily available in conventional supermarkets. Whatever brand you decide on, make sure it's certified organic; otherwise, it's likely made from GMO soybeans.

TOMATO PUREE: Use commercially processed tomatoes with minimal salt and seasonings (or none, if possible). Preferred brands: Pomi (box), Bionaturae (jar), Muir Glen (BPA-free cans).

TURNIP: Another underrated root vegetable with tremendous versatility. A little bit sweet and a little bit piquant, the turnip is the unsung hero in the gratin with blue cheese sauce (page 63). A cool-weather crop available at farmers' markets when nothing else is.

VEGETABLE STOCK: I rarely make vegetable stock anymore, mainly because my freezer space is at a premium, and I tend to need stock at the last minute. My go-to stock is now in the form of bouillon cubes from Rapunzel. I prefer the unsalted version. If you want to make your own, check out the recipe on page 214.

My go-to online suppliers and vendors are listed on page 216.

Here are a few more clarifications:

KOD: That's me referring to myself in the third person in these pages. You can call me KOD, too.

SALT: Since the publication of *The Meat Lover's Meatless Cookbook*, I've given up kosher salt, the coarse salt in the five-pound boxes from which I learned to cook professionally. Why? If I was going to be consistent on my path of cooking with less-processed ingredients, I needed to look at the processing behind an ingredient I use daily. Through Mark Bitterman, author of *Salted: A Manifesto on the World's Most Essential Mineral, with Recipes,* I learned that those five-pound boxes were 99.5 percent refined sodium chloride and that they're part of an industrial product line that includes pool salt and ice-melting aids. "It's about as close to a natural food as Velveeta is to a natural cheese," said Bitterman.

So now, I stick with salt from evaporated seawater.

UMAMI: As mentioned on page 2, this Japanese term, roughly translated as "savoriness," is considered the fifth flavor, along with sweet, sour, bitter, and salty. The best way I can describe it is the mouth-coating phenomenon and lingering finish of certain ingredients—often meat just off the fire—that make us smack our lips and say, "Wow, that's delicious." In fact, "delicious first" is part of my mission—to prove that vegetarian fare is not rabbit food. In the plant world, umami-rich ingredients with similar lip-smacking qualities include molasses, mushrooms, mustard, roasted vegetables, smoked paprika, and soy sauce.

Non-GMO

First, a definition of GMO, an acronym that stands for "genetically modified organism." More recently, you may have heard of the acronym GE, which stands for "genetically engineered" and means the same thing. In a nutshell, biotech firms are gene splicing the seeds of plants and designing genetic mutations that can tolerate herbicides.

As of this writing, GMO crops actively being produced and sold in the marketplace include canola, corn, soy, sugar beets, alfalfa, cotton, papaya, and zucchini. On the surface, it seems like a small handful, but at least 80 percent of processed and packaged food (e.g., cereal, cookies, crackers, salad dressing) on supermarket shelves contains derivatives of GE corn, canola, cotton, soy, and sugar beets. You wouldn't know it by looking at ingredient labels; instead, GMOs are disguised in the form of high-fructose corn syrup, caramel color, modified food starch, and cottonseed or soybean oil, to name a few.

The health risks associated with GE food are unclear and at the center of an ongoing controversy. Unlike the European Union, Australia, Japan, and China, the United States does not require food manufacturers to label products containing GE ingredients. As of this writing, a petition has been filed with the U.S. Food and Drug Administration to require mandatory GE-food labeling. Currently, the only way to avoid GE food is to buy certified organic. You can also look for products with the Non-GMO Project verification seal.

BASIC TO THE WHOLE THING OF BEING HUMAN IS THAT WE USE FOOD TO MARK OCCASIONS THAT ARE IMPORTANT TO US IN LIFE.

—NIGELLA LAWSON
IN *FEAST: FOOD TO CELEBRATE LIFE*

FALL

when we put the lights— and our socks—back on

AUTUMN HARVEST HOOTENANNY

Primo, the cantankerous chef in the 1996 film *Big Night* is my muse for this menu. He's butting heads with his American customers who want meatballs with their spaghetti, and sets out to present them with real Italian food (and save his restaurant) at an eponymously named feast centered around a *timpano*, a drum-shaped *torta*. Traditionally, it's flavored with a multimeat and pasta-driven filling encased in a dough shell. In place of the dough shell, I use eggplant, a vegetable usually at its peak at the bridge of summer and fall. And instead of pasta, I choose short-grain rice, inspired by Primo and his infamously perfect risotto. Early autumn is a thrilling time for produce, when the sun-kissed bumper crops of summer—tomatoes, peppers, onions, snap beans—mingle with fall pears, squash, and cruciferous greens.

EGGPLANT TIMPANO GF

This is a molded tart of sorts, with a veggie-studded tomato risotto as the filling and eggplant as the outer lining. There are three distinct components: the eggplant, the risotto, and the vegetable sauté, all of which are cooked separately and come together in a springform pan.

HERE'S WHAT YOU DO:

Eggplant Lining

Trim the stem and the bottom of each eggplant, then peel completely. Slice into ½-inch-thick strips that span the entire length of the eggplant. Lightly sprinkle with salt on one side and place on a rack to leach (release some of its water), while you work on other parts of the dish.

Preheat the oven to the BROIL setting. Line two baking sheets with parchment paper.

When ready to cook, pat the eggplant dry with paper towels.

Lightly brush both sides of the eggplant with the olive oil and arrange in a single layer on the prepared pans. Broil for 5 minutes per side. While the eggplant is cooking, lightly grease the sides and bottom of the springform pan with olive oil, then dust with the cornmeal.

Line the sides of the pan with the cooked eggplant, allowing each slice to hang over the edge. Line the bottom of the pan, overlapping as need be to cover the surface. You may need a few pieces for the top as well.

Vegetable Sauté

Heat a wide 10- or 12-inch skillet over medium heat and swirl in the oil until the surface is covered. Add the peppers and cook, stirring regularly, until slightly softened but still a little crisp, about 5 minutes. Stir in the garlic and carrots, and cook for an additional 3 minutes. Season with the oregano and salt. Remove from the heat and set aside.

▶ ▶ ▶

EGGPLANT LINING:

- 4 to 5 medium-size globe eggplants (for a total of 24 to 26 pieces)
- Salt, for leaching
- Olive oil, for greasing the eggplant and the springform pan
- Medium-grind cornmeal, for dusting the pan

VEGETABLE SAUTÉ:

- 2 tablespoons olive oil
- 3 to 4 bell peppers (any color but green), seeded and diced (about 2 cups)
- 1 to 2 cloves garlic, minced
- 1 to 2 carrots, shaved thinly with a vegetable peeler (about 1 cup)
- ½ teaspoon dried oregano
- ½ teaspoon salt

TOOLS: *10- or 12-inch skillet, parchment paper*

KITCHEN NOTES: *You can prepare both the eggplant and the risotto in advance and refrigerate until ready to assemble.*

Tomato Risotto

Keep the vegetable stock warm in a medium-size saucepan over low heat while you prepare the rest of the recipe.

In a 10- or 12-inch heavy-bottomed skillet (think wide and shallow versus tall and deep), combine the oil and butter over medium heat. Add the onion, stirring with a wooden spoon, being mindful not to let it brown, for about 3 minutes. Add the rice, coating it with the onion mixture, cooking for about 1 minute.

Pour in the wine (if using) and allow it to boil off, occasionally stirring the rice; otherwise, ladle in 1 cup of the stock and stir the rice with a wooden spoon. When the liquid is almost completely absorbed (airholes begin to appear), ladle in more stock, in ½ cup increments, stirring regularly (but not obsessively) to keep the rice from sticking and to help release its starch, for a creamy result.

In a small saucepan, combine the tomato puree and tomato paste and keep warm over low heat.

At minute 25, the rice should be about three-quarters done. Stir in the salt. Pour in the tomato mixture, increase the heat, and stir vigorously to keep the liquid from burning and for the rice to finish cooking. The rice should be creamy and firm (not mushy) and most of the liquid should be absorbed.

Turn off the heat, then stir in the Parmigiano-Reggiano.

Preheat the oven to 350°F.

Stir in the reserved vegetable sauté. Transfer the risotto to a large baking sheet and spread evenly in one layer to cool, about 15 minutes. Transfer the risotto to a bowl and stir in the smoked mozzarella.

Fill the eggplant shell with the risotto. Drape the overhanging eggplant slices over the filling. Patch any holes with extra slices. Bake for 45 minutes. Allow to rest for about 10 minutes. Remove the ring from the pan and slice with a pie cutter.

MAKES ABOUT 8 SERVINGS

TOMATO RISOTTO:

- 5 cups vegetable stock (page 214)
- 2 tablespoons olive oil
- 1 tablespoon butter (Don't do butter? Use all olive oil instead)
- ½ medium-size onion, diced very finely (about ¾ cup)
- 2 cups uncooked short-grain rice (Arborio, Carnaroli, or Vialone Nero)
- ¼ cup white wine that you enjoy drinking (optional)
- 1 cup tomato puree or marinara sauce
- 2 teaspoons tomato paste
- ½ teaspoon salt
- ½ cup grated Parmigiano-Reggiano cheese
- ½ cup thinly sliced smoked mozzarella cheese

TOOLS: *10- or 12-inch skillet*

Ingredients

- 1 (1-pound) loaf country-style bread
- ¼ cup olive oil, plus more for brushing
- 2 to 3 red bell peppers, roasted, peeled, and seeded
- Optional: Substitute 1 bell pepper for 2 dried ancho chile peppers, soaked for 1 hour, drained, seeded, and chopped roughly; or 2 fresh poblano chile peppers, roasted, peeled, and seeded
- 1 small piece fresh serrano or jalapeño pepper (½- to 1-inch long), seeded and minced
- 4 cloves garlic, minced
- ½ cup unsalted almonds and/or hazelnuts, toasted
- 2 to 3 plum tomatoes, peeled and seeded
- 2 teaspoons red wine vinegar or freshly squeezed lemon juice
- ½ teaspoon salt
- ¼ teaspoon cayenne
- ¼ teaspoon smoked paprika (optional; particularly useful in absence of poblano or ancho chile peppers)
- 6 to 8 (8- to 10-inch) leeks

TOOLS: *Food processor, parchment paper*

ROASTED LEEKS WITH ROMESCO SAUCE 🆅

Leeks are funny; you want so badly for them to be great, but left unattended, they cook unevenly and you end up with part charcoal, part raw onion. With my three-step roasting method, we should all be able to eat our leeks in tender-loving peace.

HERE'S WHAT YOU DO:

In a skillet, fry one 1-inch slice of the bread (crusts removed) in 1 tablespoon of the oil over medium heat until golden on both sides, about 5 minutes. Remove from the pan and allow to cool. Place all the peppers in a food processor, along with the garlic, nuts, and the fried bread slice. Pulse to ensure that mixture is textured, not overpureed.

Add the tomatoes, the remaining oil and vinegar. The mixture will emulsify quickly. Add the salt and cayenne, and smoked paprika, if using. If the mixture is too thick, add 1 to 2 tablespoons of water. The mixture should be both textured and fluid. Taste for salt, heat, and acid, and season accordingly.

Prepare the leeks: Cut away the dark, woody tops and slice the leeks in half lengthwise with the root intact. Wash the leeks under cold running water; silt likes to hide between layers. Remove the outermost layer of the leeks and pat the leeks dry with a kitchen towel.

Preheat the oven to 400°F. Line a baking sheet with parchment paper. Arrange the leeks in a single layer, cut side up, on the pan. Brush both sides of the leeks with olive oil, and then sprinkle the tops with salt.

Cover with foil and roast for 20 minutes. Remove the foil and roast for 5 minutes. Increase the oven heat to the BROIL setting and brown the leeks for 2 minutes.

Arrange the leeks on a platter and spoon a tablespoon of romesco sauce on top. Bring the remaining sauce to the table as well as some of the remaining bread, sliced and toasted.

Kept in an airtight container in the refrigerator, the sauce keeps for about 5 days.

MAKES ABOUT 6 SERVINGS

STIR-FRIED SNAP BEANS WITH WALNUTS GF V

- 10 cups water
- 1 teaspoon salt, plus more to taste
- 1 pound green or yellow snap beans, ends trimmed
- 1½ tablespoons olive oil
- 1 shallot bulb, peeled and diced
- ¼ cup unsalted walnuts, chopped roughly
- ¼ cup fresh mint leaves, or mixture of mint and basil, cut into a chiffonade

TOOLS: *Wok or 12-inch skillet*

Stir-frying blanched snap beans is perfectly fine but probably an unmemorable way to get your daily veg. But throwing a handful of walnuts into the mix—now we're talking. Not only do walnuts add meaty texture and mouth-coating umami, they turn an ordinary side dish into a meal. Walnuts, I've learned during the course of writing this book, are packed with good stuff. In just one-fourth of a cup (the amount called for), you get 4 grams of protein and 2 grams of fiber. But wait, there's more: The walnut is rich in both heart-healthy omega-3 fatty acids and—this is the part I love—polyphenols, those disease-fighting antioxidants the doc is always telling you about.

HERE'S WHAT YOU DO:

Bring the water to a boil in a large pot and add the salt. Add the beans and return to a boil. Cook the beans until al dente, about 6 minutes. Drain the beans and run under cold water to cool. Pat dry with a kitchen towel, then cut in half on the diagonal.

In a wok or 12-inch skillet, heat the oil over medium-high heat. Add the shallot and stir-fry, stirring frequently, about 30 seconds. Add the beans and stir and toss until the beans are coated with oil, 2 to 3 minutes. The beans may char a little; this is nice. Add the walnuts, stirring to keep them from burning, about 1 minute.

Taste the beans for salt and add more as needed. Sprinkle with the herbs and serve hot.

MAKES 6 SERVINGS

KOD'S DARK 'N' STORMY PEAR CRISP

Known as the national drink of Bermuda, the Dark 'n' Stormy is a potent potion of dark rum (traditionally, it's Gosling's Black Seal) and ginger beer, garnished with lime. It is also one of my all-time favorite cocktails. A retreat in Key West many years ago, with food-writing pal Bill Addison, was the scene of many sunset-hour sippy-poos—and of course, much contemplation on the meaning of life. Shocked back into reality with the crunch of autumn leaves and much chillier air, I was determined to re-create a little piece of paradise. To my delight, I discovered that pears like a Dark 'n' Stormy, too.

HERE'S WHAT YOU DO:

Place the raisins in a small bowl and pour the rum on top. Soak the raisins until plump, about 20 minutes.

Make the topping: In a medium-size bowl, place 6 tablespoons of the flour, 3 tablespoons of the granulated sugar, and the brown sugar, nutmeg, cinnamon, and salt. Cut 4 tablespoons of the butter into small pieces. With your fingertips, "cut" the butter into the mixture until the butter is integrated and the mixture looks like molded sand from an inverted beach pail. Add the nuts and, with your hands, mix well. It may look like a big cheese ball. Wrap in plastic and place in the refrigerator until well chilled, about 15 minutes.

Preheat the oven to 375°F.

Prep the pears: With a sharp knife, slice off the bottoms to create a flat surface, making the cutting easier and safer; then slice off the stem tops. Peel the pears. Using the core as the focal point, visualize the pear as a four-sided object. Place the blade of the knife along the fleshy side of the core of one side and slice from top to bottom for all four sides. (What should remain is the core.) Cut each section into 1-inch-thick slices.

▶ ▶ ▶

- ⅓ cup dark raisins
- ½ cup dark rum (nonalcoholic option: ½ cup brewed black tea)
- 7 tablespoons all-purpose flour
- 3 tablespoons plus 1 teaspoon granulated sugar
- 3 tablespoons light or brown sugar
- ¼ teaspoon grated nutmeg
- ½ teaspoon ground cinnamon
- ⅛ teaspoon salt
- 5 tablespoons butter, softened
- ½ cup unsalted walnuts or pecans, chopped
- 4 to 6 ripe Bartlett or Anjou pears (for a total of 5 cups)
- 3 tablespoons finely chopped crystallized ginger
- Zest of 2 limes
- Juice from 1 lime
- 1 teaspoon vanilla extract

TOOLS: *8-inch square cake pan or 9-inch pie pan*

Place the pears, ginger, lime zest, lime juice, and the remaining tablespoon of flour in a medium-size bowl and stir gently until the pears are coated. Add the raisins, along with their soaking liquid, and stir to incorporate. Sprinkle the remaining 1 teaspoon of granulated sugar all over the fruit.

Pour the filling into an 8-inch square cake pan or 9-inch pie pan.

Melt the remaining tablespoon of butter in a small saucepan over low heat. Add the vanilla extract and brown quickly, about 1 minute. (You may also do this in the microwave.) Drizzle the browned butter over the fruit.

Drop the chilled topping onto the buttered fruit, covering the entire surface. Bake until the fruit is fork tender and the topping is crunchy, 45 to 55 minutes. Let cool slightly and serve in bowls.

MAKES 6 SERVINGS

HALLOWEEN

Substantial chow always seems to get the short shrift at Halloween spookfests. If it's not a trough of candy, you'll likely be dining on a selection of glow-in-the-dark cheese-flavored puffs and crisps, followed by fake eyeball–topped cupcakes for dessert. As much as I love doing the Monster Mash, it's tough to get excited when the eats are so frightful.

Putting together a tasty yet healthful Halloween spread is easier than you think. First step: Think orange, and I mean beyond the pumpkin you plan to carve. Late October is a bonanza for vegetables in various shades of red and orange—end-of-season peppers, beets, sweet potatoes, carrots, and the endless varieties of winter squash. They are at their peak and at the ready, waiting to give you a beta-carotene boost. The options that follow will make ghouls and goblins of all ages howl with joy.

DIWALI

Known as the Hindu festival of lights, Diwali is a time of celebrating and ushering in good (light) over evil (darkness), and is usually held over several days after the autumn harvest. It is considered one of the most important holidays in India. The menu I've put together is a mix of *chaat*, the Hindi word referring to snacks, particularly of the savory and spicy variety, The dishes are served family style, on small plates, for a casual, no-tablecloth-required get-together. If you miss the Diwali boat, consider this line up for your next Oscars viewing party or a tasty excuse to catch up with friends over cocktails and/or an evening of board games.

SPICED NUTS, INDIAN STYLE GF

A make-ahead no-brainer that keeps well for weeks in an airtight jar or tin, these savory morsels fit right in at nearly any occasion, from tailgating to backyard croquet parties.

HERE'S WHAT YOU DO:

Place the fennel seeds in a skillet and toast over medium heat until slightly golden, about 90 seconds. Remove from the heat and set aside.

Then toast the coriander and cardamom seeds in the same skillet, along with the black peppercorns, until they pop and dance a little, about 2 minutes. Transfer to a coffee grinder or spice grinder and pulverize until ground.

Transfer the ground spices to a small bowl, and add the salt, brown sugar, and cayenne. Stir until well blended, then the toasted fennel seeds.

Preheat the oven to 350°F.

Place the nuts in a single layer on a baking sheet and toast for 10 minutes.

While the nuts toast, heat the oil in a microwave or in a very small saucepan on the stovetop.

Transfer the hot nuts to a large bowl and immediately drizzle the hot oil on top, followed by the spice blend, and quickly stir to toss and coat the nuts.

Serve warm or at room temperature. The nuts will keep for weeks stored in an airtight container.

MAKES ABOUT 4 CUPS

- 1 tablespoon fennel seeds
- 1 teaspoon coriander seeds
- ¼ teaspoon cardamom seeds
- ¼ teaspoon black peppercorns
- 1½ teaspoons salt
- 2 teaspoons brown sugar
- ⅛ teaspoon cayenne
- 1 pound assorted unsalted nuts (walnuts, pecans, hazelnuts, almonds, as well as peanuts, all work great)
- 1½ tablespoons neutral oil

TOOLS: *Electric coffee or spice grinder*

KITCHEN NOTES: *I recommend using whole spices and grinding them just before using, as they are more intense in flavor, really make these nuts sing, and magically perfume the house. If a spice grinder or coffee grinder–cum–spice grinder is out of the question, by all means use the ground spices.*

SPINACH PAKORAS WITH GREEN CHUTNEY GF V

GREEN CHUTNEY:

- 1 large handful fresh cilantro leaves, chopped (½ cup)
- 1 small handful fresh mint leaves, stemmed and chopped (¼ cup)
- 1 (½-inch) piece fresh ginger, peeled and chopped finely
- 1 or 2 cloves garlic, chopped
- 1 plum tomato
- 1 small green chile pepper, seeded and diced
- Salt

TOOLS: *Stand blender or food processor*

PAKORAS:

- 2 cups chickpea flour
- 2 teaspoons salt
- 1 teaspoon baking powder
- 1 teaspoon ground coriander
- ¾ teaspoon cayenne
- ½ teaspoon ground cumin
- ½ teaspoon ground turmeric
- ½ teaspoon cumin seeds (optional but nice)
- About 1½ cups cold water
- 1 bunch spinach, washed and dried thoroughly, then stemmed (4 to 5 cups)
- 2 cups neutral oil

TOOLS: *Candy thermometer; deep, heavy pot or wok; slotted spoon*

This is one of my all-time favorite snacks to make for friends, but I need to confess: For the crispiest results, you'll need to cook the *pakoras* just before serving, which means donning an apron over your party outfit. My suggestion: Serve these first and get them out of the way, or enlist a willing guest to share the workload.

HERE'S WHAT YOU DO:

Green Chutney

Combine all the ingredients except the salt in a stand blender or food processor. Blend until smooth and well mixed. Add salt to taste. Serve at room temperature.

Pakoras

Place the chickpea flour, salt, baking powder, and all of the spices in a large bowl, and stir everything together. Add the water gradually, mixing well after each addition with a rubber spatula or wooden spoon, and continue adding the water until the batter is the consistency of pancake batter. Let rest for about 15 minutes.

Meanwhile, prep the spinach: Only use leaves that are in good condition; set aside leaves that are torn or damaged. Make sure the spinach is completely dry before dipping into the batter.

Heat the oil in a deep, heavy pot or a wok until the temperature reaches 335°F. Alternatively, test the oil with a spoonful of batter, which upon contact will bubble when ready.

Arrange a few paper towels on an adjacent work surface to drain the *pakoras* after they've been fried.

Dip the spinach leaves, a few at a time, into the batter, completely coating the surface. With a pair of tongs, carefully drop the battered spinach into the hot oil and fry until golden brown and crispy on both sides, about 90 seconds. Adjust the heat as needed to minimize smoking. Remove the *pakoras* with a slotted spoon and transfer to the paper towel–lined area.

▶ ▶ ▶

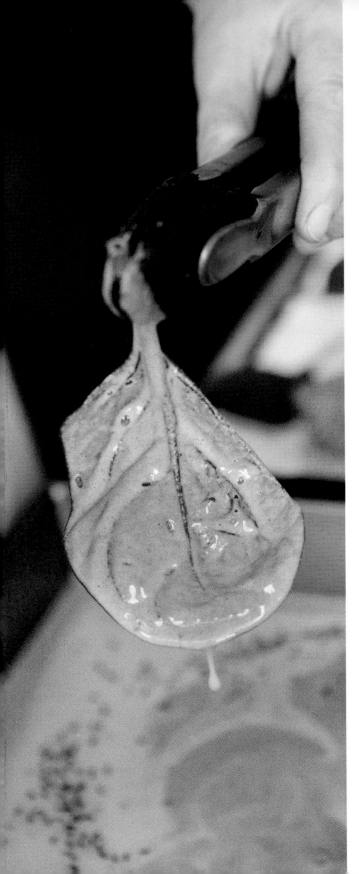

With the slotted spoon, skim any burnt bits and allow the oil to return to 335°F before adding the next batch of battered spinach.

Eat while the *pakoras* are still warm and serve with the chutney.

MAKES 6 SNACK-SIZE SERVINGS

KITCHEN NOTES: *Make the chutney first (or in advance) so that it's ready to go as the pakoras come out of the hot oil. I highly recommend that you double amounts and make a big batch of this stuff, as it's addictive and your guests will plow through it.*

BROWN RICE–PISTACHIO PILAF

GF **V**

In keeping with the Indian theme, I've scented an otherwise ordinary pilaf with a spice mélange of whole cardamom, clove, and cinnamon. As the rice cooks, the spices infuse the dish, and the house will smell heavenly. This is also a great make-ahead dish to repurpose throughout the week.

HERE'S WHAT YOU DO:

Heat a medium-size saucepan over medium-high heat and swirl in the oil until the surface is covered. Add the onion and stir to coat with the oil. Lower the heat to medium and cook until slightly softened, about 5 minutes, stirring regularly to minimize burning.

Add the rice and stir to coat with the oil and onion, about 1 minute. Add the water, plus the cinnamon stick, clove, cardamom seeds, and salt. Bring to a boil, cover, and lower the heat to low. Cook at a simmer until the water is absorbed, 40 to 45 minutes.

Feel free to remove the spices or leave them; either way is okay.

Remove from the heat, sprinkle the pistachios on top of the rice, cover, and allow to sit for 5 minutes. Serve hot.

MAKES 6 TO 8 SERVINGS

- 2 tablespoons neutral oil
- ¾ cup diced onion (a little more than ½ medium-size onion)
- 1½ cups medium- or long-grain brown rice
- 2⅔ cups water
- 1 cinnamon stick
- 1 whole clove
- ⅛ teaspoon cardamom seeds (about 3 pods' worth)
- ¾ teaspoon salt
- ⅓ cup unsalted pistachios, shelled and chopped finely

- 1 (14-ounce) package fresh extra-firm tofu, preferably organic
- 2 tablespoons peeled and minced fresh ginger (from a 2 by 2-inch hunk)
- 4 garlic cloves, minced
- ½ cup full-fat or 2% plain yogurt
- 1 tablespoon freshly squeezed lemon juice
- 2 teaspoons of your favorite curry powder
- 1 teaspoon ground cumin
- 1 teaspoon medium-heat ground chile pepper or paprika
- ¼ teaspoon cayenne (optional)
- ¼ teaspoon ground fennel
- ¼ teaspoon ground cloves
- 1 teaspoon salt
- 2 tablespoons neutral oil

TOOLS: *Eight to ten 9- or 10-inch bamboo skewers, soaked in water for 15 minutes before using; mortar and pestle, parchment paper*

TOFU TIKKA KEBABS

First, an ode to chicken tikka, a classic Indian dish of boneless chicken marinated in a highly spiced yogurt marinade and cooked on skewers in a blazing hot clay oven called a tandoor. I had a hunch that this marinade would be equally scrumptious with tofu—and I was right. This is tikka with a capital T.

HERE'S WHAT YOU DO:

Drain the tofu: Remove from the package and place on a dinner plate. Place a second plate on top of the tofu and weigh it down with a filled can or jar. Allow to sit for about 20 minutes.

Meanwhile, make the tandoori marinade: Mash the ginger and garlic until the mixture becomes pasty, preferably in a mortar and pestle. Plan B: Mince the ginger and garlic until very finely minced, the consistency of baby food.

In a medium-size bowl, combine the yogurt, ginger paste, lemon juice, curry powder, cumin, chile pepper, the cayenne (if using), fennel, cloves, and salt. Stir until well blended.

Drain off the water from the tofu. Slice the tofu in half horizontally or widthwise. Cut each half into sixteen to twenty 1-inch cubes.

Place the cubes in the marinade, stir to completely coat, and marinate in the refrigerator for about 1 hour.

Preheat the oven to 450°F and line a baking sheet with parchment paper. Remove the tofu from the marinade, patting off the excess with a paper towel. Place four cubes on each soaked skewer, with a little space in between.

Line up the skewers in a single layer on the prepared sheet. Brush the tofu with the oil; you may need to apply with a dabbing motion rather than a brush stroke.

Roast for 15 minutes. Turn the skewers onto a second side and roast for an additional 15 minutes. The tofu should be golden and sizzling.

Serve with Kicky Ketchup.

MAKES 6 SERVINGS

KICKY KETCHUP   GF V KIDDO

HERE'S WHAT YOU DO:

Place all the ingredients in a small bowl and stir together. Taste and reseason as needed. You're looking for a sauce that's piquant but not too spicy.

MAKES ABOUT 1¼ CUPS KETCHUP

- 1 cup ketchup, preferably organic
- 2 to 3 tablespoons freshly squeezed lemon juice
- ¼ teaspoon cayenne or ground chile pepper of choice
- 1 teaspoon peeled and minced fresh ginger
- Pinch of sugar

POACHED PEARS WITH SAFFRON-TEA SAUCE `GF`

- 6 medium-size, somewhat ripe Bartlett, Bosc, or Comice pears, preferably with stem
- 1 (8-ounce) cup brewed black tea of choice (brew for 5 minutes)
- 1½ cups water
- ¾ cup granulated sugar
- Zest of 1 lemon
- 1 cinnamon stick
- 6 cardamom seeds
- Pinch of saffron
- ¼ cup unsalted pistachios, shelled and chopped finely

TOOLS: *Parchment paper, 9-inch-wide saucepan*

KITCHEN NOTES: *I've done this dessert with Comice, Bosc, and Bartlett varieties and they all translate deliciously. Shucks, I bet they'd be great with Asian pears, too. It doesn't matter if the tea you use is caffeinated or not, but choose something that's robust and will carry through in the sauce.*

You may make the entire dish in advance and refrigerate until 30 minutes before serving. Gently reheat the sauce.

Food writer and cookbook author Monica Bhide graciously brainstormed with me on flavor notes of her native India. I owe her a tray of these pears inspired by her spiced wisdom.

HERE'S WHAT YOU DO:

You'll need a saucepan that's at least 9 inches wide. Trace the outline of the pan on parchment paper and cut out the circle. Set aside.

Peel the pears and trim the bottoms so they stand upright. With a paring knife, core the pears from the bottom, carefully scraping away the seeds in a screwdriver fashion.

Place the tea, water, and sugar in the saucepan. Over medium heat, bring to a quick boil, and add the lemon zest, cinnamon stick, cardamom, and saffron. Lower the heat to low and add the pears. They should be able to sit upright, but as they cook, they may wobble on their sides; that's okay.

Place the prepared parchment circle on top of the pears and cut a hole in the middle so that the parchment will lay flat. Lay a small, heatproof plate on top of the paper, then cover the pan.

Over medium-low heat, cook the pears for 15 minutes, remove the plate and parchment, and check on the pears' progress and liquid level. The pears are done when a paring knife easily glides into their sides. Otherwise, replace the parchment, plate, and lid, and cook for an additional 10 to 15 minutes. With tongs or a slotted spoon, remove the pears from the pan and transfer to a plate.

Remove the lemon zest and cinnamon stick. Transfer the sauce to a small saucepan and bring to a boil. Cook over medium-heat until the sauce is reduced by more than half, about 30 minutes. The sauce will have the consistency of maple syrup.

Serve the pears at room temperature. Drizzle the warm sauce over each pear and garnish with chopped pistachios.

MAKES 6 SERVINGS

ELECTION NIGHT

Before moving to Seattle, my husband and I had been longtime residents of the Washington, D.C., area, where presidential election night nail biting is considered something of a sport. Every four years on the first Tuesday in November, folks from all corners of the Beltway come out of the woodwork and gather 'round a television screen to speculate, gesticulate, and cheer for their candidate as if it were a football game. Unlike athletes of other sports, election night nail biters miss the boat on marathon endurance chow and inevitably have a pizza delivered, hardly the stuff of stamina.

We didn't know it then, but November 4, 2008, was more than the night that Barack Obama was declared the presidential victor. It marked the beginning of a conversation in which politics, policy, food, and health would take center stage. No one could predict that Michelle Obama would keep reporters busy covering the First Lady's myriad food-and-health initiatives, from Let's Move! to the White House kitchen garden, the first of its kind since World War II. If nothing else, the First Lady has reignited a long-ignored conversation about the state of the union's diet.

My hope is that no matter who lives in the White House, we continue to look outside the (pizza) box for sustenance and inspiration (and celebrations!). These suggested eat-while-you-view options can all be made in advance, so you don't have to miss a nail-biting moment.

THANKSGIVING

As I rewind the reel of "It's Your Life: Thanksgiving Edition," certain images emerge: Aunt Ginny's enthusiastic use of Kitchen Bouquet, a brown liquid in a little brown bottle, which was always added to the gravy. The bag of Parker House rolls, warmed up in its very own aluminum tray. The always lapped-up green bean casserole with the fried onion bits out of a can. Stuffing from a box and the ritual of hanging the wishbone out to dry for the kids to pull. After dinner, there would be a pinochle game in the basement and a lively kind of mayhem that comes when twenty people with the same gene pool gather under one roof.

Many years and boxes of stuffing later, I would proudly whip up my first batch of homemade cranberry sauce, stirring at the stove with my kid brother Tim, and one year, I got fancy and flambéed the turkey without burning the house down. But it isn't really the food that I remember about Thanksgivings past; it's the feeling. It's part of my life story as told through one meal, as I'm sure it is for you.

There's nothing hunted on this menu, but plenty of the farmers' market–foraged, including gratinéed sweet potatoes, Brussels sprouts slaw style, and apples teamed up with rosemary in my newfangled pie dough. You had better believe this is a harvest celebration.

DELICATA BOATS
WITH RED RICE STUFFING GF V

Stuffed acorn squash: the intentions are always good, but unfortunately, the results rarely live up to the hype. Fortunately, there's another way to meatless main dish happiness, people! It comes in the form of the delicata squash, a thin-skinned, quick-cooking variety that tastes like a mash-up of corn and sweet potatoes. Stuffed with mahogany-hued red rice, these boats are hearty yet elegant and actually taste like the squash of our dreams.

HERE'S WHAT YOU DO:

Bring the water and the rice to a boil in a medium-size saucepan. Lower the heat to low, cover, and cook at a simmer, 20 to 25 minutes. The rice will be done when water is absorbed and grains are tender to the bite. (Kept covered for 5 to 10 minutes, the rice will continue to cook.)

Preheat the oven to 400°F and line a baking sheet with parchment paper.

Trim both ends of each squash and slice in half lengthwise. Scoop out and discard the seeds and the attached pulp. Brush both sides of the squash with the olive oil, and season the inside to taste with salt and pepper.

Roast until easily pierced with a fork, about 30 minutes, and remove from the oven. Lower the oven heat to 350°F.

While the squash roasts, make the filling: Transfer the rice to a large mixing bowl and add the ⅛ cup of olive oil, and the parsley, nuts, dried fruit, fennel seeds, ginger, citrus zest, and chile pepper. Stir until the rice is coated with the oil and the mixture is well mixed. Add the ¼ teaspoon of salt, stir, taste, and reseason if necessary.

Fill each squash half with about ¼ cup of the filling. Return to the oven and heat for about 15 minutes, until the rice is warmed through.

Serve immediately, or lower the oven temperature to 225°F, cover with foil, and hold until ready to serve.

MAKES 6 TO 8 SERVINGS

- 1½ cups water

- 1 cup Bhutanese red rice (Plan B: long-grain Wehani; cooking times and liquid amounts may vary)

- 3 to 4 delicata squash (about 1 pound each)

- ⅛ cup olive oil, plus extra for brushing

- ¼ teaspoon salt, plus more to taste

- Freshly ground black pepper

- ½ cup fresh flat-leaf parsley, chopped

- ¼ cup unsalted shelled pistachios, chopped (Other options: walnuts, almonds, or pecans, also chopped)

- ⅓ cup dried cranberries or cherries, chopped

- 1 teaspoon fennel seeds

- 1 teaspoon peeled and minced fresh ginger

- Zest of ½ lemon or orange, plus 1 or 2 squeezes of the juice

- ⅛ teaspoon ground chile pepper of choice

TOOLS: *Parchment paper*

KITCHEN NOTES: *There's enough filling for eight servings (one squash half per person). For a party of six, you'll have more than a cup of remaining filling, which you can bring to the table.*

ROASTED RED ONIONS WITH PUMPKIN-ROSEMARY STUFFING AND ROOT VEGETABLE GRAVY

A multistep, time-consuming affair this dish may be, but every-thing can be made in staggered fashion over the course of two days and assembled when you're ready to serve. Your labor will result in a beauty of a dish: red onion shells now a shade of mauve, filled with all the colors of autumn in the pumpkin bread stuffing. The guests will go wild.

DAY ONE

ROOT VEGETABLE GRAVY

This is no gravy in the ordinary sense, in that there are no pan drip-pings or roux to speak of. A mess of root vegetables are slathered with olive oil and roasted until super tender, then pureed and thinned out with vegetable stock. Thanks to my ingenious friend Nicole Aloni, who's got a slew of cookbooks under her own belt, I learned this handy trick, which turns a rouxless sauce into a gravy with gusto.

HERE'S WHAT YOU DO:

Preheat the oven to 425°F. Line a roasting pan with parchment paper.

Place all the vegetables, shallots, and garlic in a large bowl and add 2 tablespoons of the olive oil. With your hands, coat the vegetables with the oil. Season with the salt.

Arrange the vegetables in a single layer in the prepared pan and roast for 35 minutes. Check on the garlic; if very soft to the touch, remove. (You do not want it to burn.) Cover the pan and roast the vegetables for an additional 10 minutes; they should be tender enough to cut with a fork.

Remove the now-cooled garlic cloves from their skins and place in the bowl of a food processor, along with the roasted vegetables and thyme. Process until well blended; the mixture will resemble a puree. While the motor is running, add the remaining 2 tablespoons of olive oil. The mixture should be smooth and free of vegetable bits.

ROOT VEGETABLE GRAVY:

- 1 medium-size onion, halved and peeled

- 2 cups peeled, 2- to 3-inch pieces of any combination of parsnips, carrots, or celery root

- 1 shallot bulb, peeled and left whole

- 6 cloves garlic, skin on

- 4 tablespoons olive oil

- ¼ teaspoon salt

- 1½ teaspoons fresh thyme, or 1 teaspoon dried

- 3 to 5 cups vegetable stock (page 214)

- 2 teaspoons soy sauce or wheat-free tamari

- Freshly ground black pepper

- ½ lemon

TOOLS: *Roasting pan, parchment paper, food processor*

KITCHEN NOTES: *I've created a two-day game plan to divide the workload and help manage prep among the dish's four main components.*

The gravy can be made in advance and gently reheated when ready to serve. You can make your own vegetable stock, as detailed on page 214, or you can make it from Rapunzel brand of unsalted bouillon cubes, which have become my go-to stock.

In a medium-size saucepan over low heat, warm the vegetable stock and keep at a simmer.

Pour the puree into another medium-size saucepan and heat over medium heat. Gradually ladle in the stock until it arrives at the desired consistency; I'm usually happy with the results after 3 cups of stock. Season with the soy sauce (this will also give the gravy a little color à la Kitchen Bouquet).

Generously season with the black pepper to taste, and a faint squeeze of the lemon. Keep on the heat until ready to pour into a gravy boat.

To make ahead: Let cool, then store in the refrigerator until ready to reheat for serving.

MAKES 1 QUART GRAVY

PUMPKIN-ROSEMARY STUFFING

This stuffing is inspired by a pumpkin-raisin quick bread from a Bobby Flay cookbook. It's the foundation for Flay's bread pudding, which I made for several consecutive Thanksgivings. With the exception of a smidge of sugar, the quick bread for the stuffing is seriously savory, with freshly chopped rosemary leading the charge.

HERE'S WHAT YOU DO:

Grease a 9-inch loaf pan and preheat the oven to 350°F.

In a medium-size bowl, combine the flour, baking powder, baking soda, sugar, all of the ground spices, and salt and stir together.

Using a stand or handheld mixer, cream the butter with the sugar in a large bowl until fluffy, about 90 seconds. Add the oil and egg and beat until somewhat frothy, another 90 seconds. Then add the yogurt and the pumpkin puree and beat until well mixed.

Add the dry ingredients, in thirds, alternating with the water, to the wet batter. With a rubber spatula or wooden spoon, mix together. The batter will be somewhat sticky. Stir in the dried fruit and rosemary until evenly distributed.

Scoop the batter into the prepared pan, place on a baking sheet, and bake for 65 to 75 minutes, or until a skewer inserted in the middle comes out clean. The top of the bread should spring back when pressed lightly.

▶ ▶ ▶

PUMPKIN-ROSEMARY STUFFING:

- Oil or butter, for greasing a loaf pan
- 1¾ cups all-purpose flour
- 1 teaspoon baking powder
- ¼ teaspoon baking soda
- 1 teaspoon ground cinnamon
- ½ teaspoon ground ginger
- ¼ teaspoon ground cloves
- ¾ teaspoon salt
- 4 tablespoons butter, softened and cut into several pieces
- 1 tablespoon granulated sugar
- ¼ cup neutral oil
- 1 egg
- ⅓ cup full-fat or 2% plain yogurt, ideally Greek style
- 1 cup unsweetened pure pumpkin puree (from a 15-ounce can)
- ½ cup water
- ½ cup dried cranberries, cherries, or currants
- 1 tablespoon fresh rosemary, chopped finely

TOOLS: *Stand or handheld mixer, 9-inch loaf pan*

PREP THE ONIONS AND MAKE THE STUFFING:

- 7 red onions (about ½ pound each)
- 6 cups water
- 2 tablespoons olive oil
- 1 cup finely chopped celery (2 to 3 stalks) or bok choy
- 2 cloves garlic, minced
- 2 cups Swiss chard or spinach that has been washed, dried, stemmed and finely chopped
- Large pinch of ground chile pepper of choice
- Salt and freshly ground black pepper
- 1 to 2 cups vegetable stock (page 214)
- Pumpkin-rosemary bread cubes (page 47)

TOOLS: *Melon baller, 12-inch skillet*

Place the pan on a rack and let cool for 15 minutes. Run a knife along the sides of the pan and invert to release the bread, and let cool completely on the rack.

When the bread is completely cooled, cut into 1-inch cubes. Place the cubes on a baking sheet in a single layer and allow to dry out overnight. If the cubes need additional toasting, place in the oven at 300°F for up to an hour.

MAKES 6 TO 7 CUPS BREAD CUBES

DAY TWO/DAY OF SERVING
PREP THE ONIONS AND MAKE THE STUFFING

HERE'S WHAT YOU DO:

Trim the tops and bottoms of six of the onions so they can sit upright, then peel. With a melon baller or a teaspoon, dig a little well in the top of each onion to create an opening, without tunneling through.

Place the onions in a medium-size saucepan, along with the water. Bring to a boil and cook for 20 minutes over medium heat.

Preheat the oven to 425°F.

Transfer the cooked onions to a baking dish and add a small amount of the cooking liquid—about ½ cup—until the surface of the dish is covered. Cover with foil and roast for 45 minutes.

While the onions roast, make the stuffing: Cut the remaining red onion in half, peel, and mince; you're looking for a total of ½ cup.

Heat the olive oil in a 12-inch skillet over medium-high heat. Add the minced red onion, celery, and garlic, stirring regularly until slightly softened, about 4 minutes. Add the chard and turn with tongs until coated with the aromatics. Cook until the greens wilt, 2 to 3 minutes. Season with the chile pepper, and salt and black pepper to taste.

Meanwhile, bring the vegetable stock to a quick boil in a medium-size saucepan, then lower the heat to low, keeping it hot at a gentle simmer.

Place the rosemary-pumpkin bread cubes in a large bowl. Place the contents of the skillet mixture on top, and mix together until well mixed. Ladle in the hot stock in ½-cup increments, keeping an eye on absorption. Be careful not to oversaturate the stuffing, yielding a soggy result. Taste for seasonings and add salt and pepper as needed.

With tongs, remove the onions one by one from the baking dish and transfer to a plate. Drain them of any lingering water and set aside until cool enough to handle. Drain the baking dish of the water.

Lower the oven temperature to 350°F. Lightly grease a baking dish.

Pushing from the top opening, remove each onion's insides. (You can store the onion remnants in the refrigerator for fried rice or your next omelet; they will keep for a few days in a covered container.) It's okay if a hole results on the other end. Carefully return the onion shells to the baking dish. Fill the onions with the stuffing until generously packed, and put the remaining stuffing in the prepared baking dish.

Cover the onions with foil and bake until warmed through, about 15 minutes. Make room for the remaining stuffing, also covered with foil, and bake until hot, about 20 minutes.

Serve with the root vegetable gravy.

MAKES 6 SERVINGS

MAPLE CRANS `GF` `V`

Hands down, a pot of cranberry sauce is the easiest thing on this menu. It's so easy and quick—30 minutes from start to finish—that I even recommend it for procrastinating stress kitties. I know some folks at your table may request the can o' jelly, but don't let that stop you from whipping up a batch of the DIY sauce. The nonbelievers won't believe what they've been missing.

HERE'S WHAT YOU DO:

Rinse the cranberries and place in a medium-size saucepan. Using a zester or grater, remove the zest of one of the oranges, dice, and add to the saucepan. Slice both oranges in half and squeeze the juice over the cranberries. You want enough liquid to barely cover the cranberries; add water as necessary.

Add ¾ cup of the maple syrup, reserving the rest to use as needed. Stir the mixture until well mixed and bring to a boil.

Lower the heat and cook at a simmer; cranberries will make a popping noise as they cook, reduce, and thicken. Stir occasionally and cook until they reach desired consistency. Taste for the sweet/tart ratio and add more maple syrup as necessary. The cranberries will be ready in as little as 25 minutes.

Serve either warm or at room temperature.

MAKES ABOUT 2½ CUPS CRANBERRIES

- 1 pound fresh cranberries, washed thoroughly
- 2 oranges
- 8 ounces good-quality pure maple syrup, or to taste

KITCHEN NOTES: *I'm lucky to live in a state where cranberries grow, so in October and the weeks leading up to Thanksgiving, I can get them at my local farmers' market. Given their short season, I stock up and stow crans in my freezer, making enough for Thanksgiving, then "putting up" the rest in jars for the months beyond. Below, I've got you covered to satisfy both immediate and delayed gratification.*

Can be made days in advance and either frozen or refrigerated in an airtight container for 5 days.

To preserve the cranberries in jars: I've detailed the steps for canning cranberries, along with other seasonal produce, in the preserved pantry section on page 21.

SWEET POTATO–PESTO GRATIN

 GF DO KIDDO

KALE PESTO:

- 4 cups water
- 1 to 1½ teaspoons salt
- 4 to 5 cups lacinato (a.k.a. dinosaur or Tuscan) kale that has been stemmed and chopped coarsely (1 large bunch)
- 2 cloves garlic, peeled and sliced
- ¼ cup unsalted walnuts, coarsely chopped
- ½ cup olive oil
- ½ cup grated Parmigiano-Reggiano cheese (optional)
- Freshly ground black pepper

TOOLS: *Blender or food processor*

SWEET POTATO GRATIN:

- Olive oil or oil spray, for greasing
- 2 pounds sweet potatoes, washed and peeled
- ½ cup kale pesto
- ⅛ to ¼ cup grated Parmigiano-Reggiano or pecorino cheese (optional)

TOOLS: *13 by 9-inch baking dish*

This is such a nice change of pace from the iconic marshmallow-engulfed variation that has graced Thanksgiving tables for decades. Imagine, a sweet potato dish that won't give you a sugar high! Instead, the thinly sliced tubers are slathered up with my beloved kale pesto, a green spread with both gusto and all-purpose prowess (it's also featured with the Stromboli (83) and the Jumbo Pasta Shells with Kale Pesto and White Beans (125).

HERE'S WHAT YOU DO:

Kale Pesto

Bring the water to a boil in a medium-size saucepan. Add 1 teaspoon of the salt, then add the kale. Cook uncovered until tender, about 10 minutes. Drain the kale under cold running water. With your hands, squeeze as much water out of the kale as possible; you'll end up with a green ball about the size of a tennis ball.

In a blender or food processor, combine the garlic and walnuts, and whiz until pulverized and well mixed. Add the kale and process until well blended; the mixture may even look a little dry. Pour in the oil and blend. The mixture should be glistening and will have a consistency that is somewhat textured, somewhat loose. Taste and add the remaining ½ teaspoon of salt, if needed.

Transfer the pesto to a small bowl and stir in the cheese (if using) and the black pepper to taste.

The pesto keeps well in an airtight container in the refrigerator, for up to a week.

MAKES ABOUT 1 CUP PESTO

Sweet Potato Gratin

Preheat the oven to 400°F.

Grease the bottom of a 13 by 9-inch baking dish with the olive oil (using a brush) or with oil spray.

Cut the sweet potato into ¼-inch-thick slices. Place in a medium-size bowl and add the pesto, stirring until the sweet potato slices are completely coated. If the coverage is light, add a wee bit more pesto, in 1-teaspoon increments.

Arrange the sweet potato slices in the prepared dish in overlapping fashion. You will have two or three layers when you're done.

If using the cheese, sprinkle evenly on top.

Cover the dish with foil and bake for 45 minutes. Remove the foil and bake for an additional 15 to 20 minutes, or until fork tender.

Serve hot.

MAKES 6 SIDE-DISH SERVINGS

KITCHEN NOTES: *Sweet potatoes can be large and unwieldy and sometimes difficult to cut. Sharpen your knife and cut the sweet potato in half, both in length and width, if necessary.*

Make the pesto first. In fact, you can make it in advance, as it keeps for several days in the refrigerator.

On prepping the kale: Grab the thick fibrous stem running through the middle and simply pull off the leafy part. You can also run a knife along the middle and trim the leaf away from the stem.

HOT BRUSSELS SPROUTS SLAW
GF **V**

- 1½ pounds Brussels sprouts, washed and stem ends trimmed
- 1 medium-size apple of choice
- 4 tablespoons olive oil
- 2 cloves garlic, sliced thinly
- ¼ cup of a white wine you enjoy drinking
- 1 teaspoon smoked paprika
- 1 teaspoon salt
- ¾ teaspoon dried thyme
- Juice of ½ lemon

TOOLS: *12-inch skillet*

In the absence of bacon, which is commonly paired with these diminutive cabbages, I add smoked paprika for another layer of flavor and a hit of umami. Feel free to omit if it's not your thing or it's not in the cupboard.

This dish comes together in mere minutes and can be done when everything else on your Thanksgiving menu is ready to go.

HERE'S WHAT YOU DO:
With a sharp knife, cut the Brussels sprouts in half, then into thin slices. Some pieces will already look shredded; others will remain leafy and will need to be sliced further. Remember, you're looking for the makings of slaw. Peel the apple and thinly slice off its top and bottom. Using the core as your focal point, visualize the apple as a four-sided object. Place the blade of your knife on the fleshy edge of the core and slice from top to bottom. You should have four equal pieces, with only the core remaining. Slice each piece into thin matchsticks and set aside.

Heat the oil in a 12-inch skillet over medium-high heat. Add the Brussels sprouts in batches, along with the garlic, constantly turning with tongs to coat with the oil and facilitate wilting. This will take about 8 minutes.

Pour in the wine, stirring the vegetables for even coverage. Allow the wine to come to a quick boil, then lower the heat, add the smoked paprika, salt, and thyme, and turn to coat the vegetables with the seasonings. Stir in the sliced apple and let it mix with the other ingredients, about 2 minutes.

Squeeze the lemon juice over the slaw, stir, and transfer to a serving bowl. Eat hot.

MAKES 6 SERVINGS

APPLE-ROSEMARY-WALNUT PIE WITH ENLIGHTENED PIE DOUGH

Forget everything you've ever learned about pie dough (except, of course, that you're the boss and the dough knows when you're afraid). As part of my goal to lighten up dessert, I consulted my friend Kate McDermott, a Seattle-based teacher and pie Bodhisattva, to develop a more healthful makeover of the all-butter crust that so many of us grew up with.

Our recipe is a fifty-fifty butter–olive oil blend, using an unorthodox combination of techniques that includes the hot water method traditionally used for meat pies in England and a "letter" fold that encourages the flaky layers reminiscent of a butter crust. The dough cooperates best when about body temperature, a stark departure from the traditional all-butter crust, which is typically very cold.

HERE'S WHAT YOU DO:

Apple-Rosemary-Walnut Filling

Peel the apples and thinly slice off their tops and bottoms. Using the core as your focal point, visualize each apple as a four-sided object. Place the blade of your knife on the fleshy edge of the core and slice from top to bottom. You should have four equal pieces, with only the core remaining. Cut into slices about ¼-inch thick, and place in a medium-size bowl. Add the remaining ingredients and stir until well mixed and evenly distributed. Set aside until you are ready to fill the dough-lined pan.

Enlightened Pie Dough

Place the olive oil in a small bowl and set aside.

Place the water in a small saucepan and heat until very hot. It need not be boiling but should be pretty close.

While the water is heating, measure out the flour. Remove 1½ tablespoons and reserve for rolling out the dough. (You may need more than

▶ ▶ ▶

APPLE-ROSEMARY-WALNUT FILLING:

- 3 to 4 apples of your choice (for a total of 3 cups)

- 2 tablespoons cornstarch, preferably organic (Plan B: arrowroot)

- ¼ to ⅓ cup granulated sugar, to taste

- 1½ teaspoons fresh rosemary, chopped finely

- ¼ teaspoon salt

- ½ cup unsalted walnuts, chopped

- Juice of ½ lemon

KITCHEN NOTES: *Make the filling first so that it's ready to go as soon as the dough is rolled out. As for the dough, have all the ingredients at the ready and measured before you get started.*

I recommend using a silicone baking mat or brown parchment paper as the rolling surface. Either one is temperature neutral and helps to keep your beautiful dough from sticking. If all you have in the house is plastic wrap, use that. If you've got a love affair with your marble countertop, go for it.

ENLIGHTENED PIE DOUGH:

- 6 tablespoons olive oil

- ½ cup water

- 3 cups all-purpose flour, at room temperature, plus more for dusting

- ¼ teaspoon plus ⅛ teaspoon salt

- ¼ teaspoon plus ⅛ teaspoon baking powder

- 6 tablespoons cold butter, cut into tablespoon-size pieces

- Egg white wash: 1 egg white, beaten with 1 tablespoon of water

- Granulated sugar, for sprinkling

TOOLS: *Food processor, rolling pin, 5-inch dough scraper, silicone baking mat or parchment paper, ruler or measuring tape, 9-inch pie pan*

your reserve, for rolling.) Place in a food processor, along with the salt and baking powder. Pulse a few times just to mix.

Add the butter. Pulse until the mixture looks and feels like fluffy sand. You should not be able to see butter clumps.

Measure out 6 tablespoons of the hot water and add to the oil. With a fork, whisk together; it will look like a vinaigrette.

Pour the oil mixture on top of the flour mixture, and pulse until the dough just comes together. It may slightly pull away from the sides of the bowl. The dough should feel soft, warm, and pliable, not hard and crumbly. If the dough looks as if it needs more liquid, add the hot water in 1-tablespoon increments, pulse, and check the softness of the dough.

Lightly dust your rolling surface with some of the reserved flour and place the dough on top. Surround the dough with both hands to let it know you're there, or as Kate says, "give it a good handshake," molding it into a thick, cohesive lump.

Roll the dough in quick, even strokes, making a quarter-turn after every few strokes. As you rotate and roll the dough, check regularly to make sure the dough is not sticking. (The dough scraper is helpful at this stage.) The immediate goal is to make a rectangle roughly 9 by 11-inches. (Don't worry if it's not exact.)

Fold the dough like a letter: Starting from a short edge, fold over a third of your dough. Take the opposite edge and fold it to the middle, covering the first fold.

Make a quarter-turn, then roll out the dough into a new rectangle, dusting with flour as needed.

Make another letter fold with dough. Give the dough another quarter-turn and roll the dough in all four directions—north, south, east, west. Fold the dough in half into a 4- to 5-inch square packet. Roll lightly on the top to seal the layers and surround the edges with both hands to tidy the dough.

Cut the dough in half, wrap each in plastic, and allow to rest in the refrigerator for 10 minutes. Unlike an all-butter dough, this dough never goes into a deep sleep and gets cold; think of it as a brief catnap after all that rolling and folding.

Meanwhile, preheat the oven to 425°F.

Lightly dust the rolling surface and roll out one dough half. With more of those quick, even strokes, roll the dough into a circle until it's about 1 inch larger than your pie pan.

Fold the dough in half and transfer to the pie pan. (Use the dough scraper to help with the lifting.)

Press the dough into the pan, making sure that it's completely covered. Trim any overhanging dough with kitchen shears or a paring knife and reserve for possible patchwork on the top layer.

Fill the lined pan with the prepared fruit mixture.

Roll out the remaining dough half in the same manner, and fold in half to transfer and lay on top of the filling. Carefully unfold the dough to cover the entire filling. Make sure that the edges of the top and bottom dough layers meet before you trim any overhanging dough with kitchen shears or a paring knife. Use any extra dough to patch holes or tears.

Make a few slashes on the top of the dough with a paring knife. (I like to make four or five in a circular pattern in the center; feel free to get creative.)

Brush with the egg white wash, then sprinkle lightly with the sugar. Transfer the pie to the refrigerator for a quick 5-minute chill.

Place on a baking sheet and bake for 5 minutes. Lower heat to 400°F and bake for an additional 50 to 55 minutes. The crust will be golden and the filling will bubble.

Remove the pie from the baking sheet and let cool on a rack for about 90 minutes so that the filling can set.

MAKES A DOUBLE-CRUST 9-INCH PIE

PUMPKIN PUDDING WITH MOLASSES COOKIES

PUMPKIN PUDDING:

- 1 (12-ounce) package firm silken tofu, preferably organic or non-GMO
- 1 (15-ounce) can unsweetened pure pumpkin puree
- 1 teaspoon vanilla extract
- ¾ cup granulated sugar
- ¼ teaspoon salt
- 1 to 2 teaspoons ground cinnamon
- ¾ teaspoon ground ginger
- ¼ teaspoon ground cloves

TOOLS: *Food processor or stand blender*

KITCHEN NOTES: *For some, 1 teaspoon of cinnamon will be plenty, but I added the option of even more for those who are nostalgic for lots of cinnamon with their pumpkin puree.*

Procrastinators take note: This one is for you. Here's a fun alternative to pumpkin pie that takes all of 15 minutes to put together. While the pudding chills, you can make a batch of molasses cookies, which can be baked in small, last-minute slice-and-bake fashion. FYI: The pudding is vegan (although no one will be able to tell), but the cookies are not.

HERE'S WHAT YOU DO:

Pumpkin Pudding

Place the tofu, with its liquid, and pumpkin puree in the bowl of a food processor or in a stand blender and puree until well blended. Add the vanilla, sugar, salt, 1 teaspoon of the cinnamon, and the ginger and cloves.

Process until well blended, then taste for cinnamon. Does it need more? Add accordingly and blend again as needed.

Pour the pudding into a bowl, cover with plastic, and chill for at least an hour, until cold and slightly firm.

Serve cold in dessert bowls, with Molasses Cookies. Leftovers keep well for a few days in an airtight container. The pudding may separate slightly, easily remedied by a few stirs.

MAKES 3½ CUPS PUDDING, AT LEAST 6 SERVINGS

HERE'S WHAT YOU DO:

Molasses Cookies

Place the flour, baking soda, baking powder, salt, cinnamon, ginger, and cloves in a medium-size mixing bowl, and mix together with a rubber spatula or scraper.

With a stand or handheld mixer, cream the butter with the sugar until well blended and fluffy. Add the oil, followed by the egg, and mix until blended thoroughly. Then add the molasses and vanilla, mixing until just incorporated.

▶ ▶ ▶

MOLASSES COOKIES:

- 2 cups all-purpose flour, plus more for dusting
- ½ teaspoon baking soda
- ½ teaspoon baking powder
- ½ teaspoon salt
- 1 teaspoon ground cinnamon
- 1½ teaspoons ground ginger
- ⅛ teaspoon ground cloves
- 4 tablespoons butter, softened and cut into several pieces
- ⅔ cup light or dark brown sugar
- ¼ cup neutral oil, plus more for sugar-coating the cookies
- 1 egg
- ¼ cup unsulfured blackstrap molasses
- 1 teaspoon vanilla extract
- 1 tablespoon very hot water or brewed black coffee
- Granulated or raw sugar, for coating cookies

TOOLS: *Stand or handheld mixer, parchment paper, 5-inch dough scraper*

KITCHEN NOTES: *Lightly grease a measuring cup before adding the molasses, as it likes to stick.*

For more decorative effect, use sugar that's coarser than granulated. It need not be fancy; turbinado (a.k.a. raw) sugar, readily available in conventional supermarkets, has larger crystals that really sparkle on top of the cookies.

Stir in the dry ingredients by hand: Add the dry ingredients, in thirds, to the wet batter, using a rubber spatula or scraper. Add the hot liquid in between the first and second dry addition. The batter may look as if it needs more liquid, but resist the temptation and give it a few more turns with the spatula until the dry flecks disappear. In fact, the dough will end up sticky and soft.

Lightly dust a silicone baking mat or parchment paper with flour, as well as your hands. Scoop the dough onto your work surface, mold into a cohesive lump, and with the dough scraper, cut the dough into four equal pieces. Shape each piece into a log 5 to 6 inches long and wrap in plastic wrap. Roll the wrapped logs into a more cylindrical shape. Refrigerate for about 1 hour, until well chilled. Note: The dough can be frozen at this stage. When ready to use, thaw in the refrigerator before baking.

Preheat the oven to 350°F. Line two baking sheets with parchment paper. Pour about ¼ cup of the granulated sugar into a saucer, for coating the cookies.

Remove a dough log from the refrigerator, and while still covered in plastic, roll to remove any flat edges. Remove the plastic, and with a serrated knife, cut into disks about ½ inch thick. Arrange on the prepared pans, leaving a few inches of space between rows.

Smear a teaspoon of the oil on the bottom of a drinking glass, then dip the glass into the sugar. Press the sugar-coated glass bottom onto each dough disk, to flatten. Dip the glass into the sugar, one by one, for each dough disk. Grease the glass once per dough log.

Bake for about 10 minutes and transfer to a cooling rack, where the cookies will quickly crisp. The cookies keep best in a metal tin or glass jar.

MAKES ABOUT 5 DOZEN COOKIES

WINTER

**when the nights are long
and so are the pajamas**

WARMING UP TO WINTER WINGDING

Just as you're finishing up Thanksgiving leftovers, December arrives, all jacked up with a ton of places to go. Whether or not you celebrate Hanukkah, Christmas, or Kwanzaa, chances are your calendar is packed with various potlucks, cookie exchanges, eggnog drop-bys, and all the other words for *party* in the thesaurus. There's winter solstice—and don't forget Festivus! The feedbag is endless. Your next invitation is one to stay at home, perhaps with a roaring fire or Vince Guaraldi on the speakers, to whip up a homespun spread that features root vegetables, winter citrus, and hearty greens. The two dessert options, by the way, make great gifts. Just sayin'.

POTATO-TURNIP GRATIN WITH BLUE CHEESE SAUCE

A stack of starchy root vegetables bathing in blue cheese sauce. By my estimation, this gratin is probably among the richest dishes in the collection, but I've done my darnedest to lighten up on the cheese and other dairy to minimize the stomach-bomb effect. I love how the turnips keep the easily squashed spuds on their toes, lending piquant notes and texture to what can often be a one-dimensional dish. During the darkest time of the year, this dish has a way of warming up the room and lightening our mood.

HERE'S WHAT YOU DO:

Have ready a medium-size bowl or container filled with water.

Thoroughly scrub and peel the potatoes and turnips and place in the water-filled bowl. Working one at a time, slice each potato and turnip in half so that you have two pieces that are flush with your cutting surface. With a sharp knife, cut into slices about ¼-inch thick and return them to the water until ready to assemble entire dish. The water helps minimize browning (and yes, you can do this step the day before).

Bring the water to a boil in a medium-size saucepan. Drain the vegetables and add to the boiling water in two batches. Parboil for 5 minutes. Remove the vegetables with tongs or a spider strainer and transfer to a bowl. Return the water to a boil if necessary and add the remaining vegetables, for a 5-minute parboil.

Generously grease all sides of a 9-inch square or 10 by 7-inch rectangular baking dish.

Make a roux: In a medium-size saucepan, melt the butter over medium heat, then stir in the flour with a wooden spoon. The mixture will cling together, and as it warms, it will quickly loosen and look slightly oozy. Stir until you see little bubbles, making sure not to burn the roux.

Now make a béchamel sauce: Pour the milk into the roux, increase the heat to medium-high, and stir regularly to prevent scalding. Within minutes, the milk will thicken and look more saucelike. French classicists will argue that the sauce is ready when your finger creates a

▶ ▶ ▶

- 6 cups total potatoes and turnips (I'm partial to a 4 to 2 ratio of potatoes to turnips, which translates to 4 medium-size potatoes and 1 medium-large turnip)
- 6 cups water
- Oil or butter, for greasing baking dish
- 3 tablespoons butter
- 3 tablespoons all-purpose flour
- 2½ cups whole or 2% milk
- 1 teaspoon salt
- ⅛ teaspoon paprika or medium-heat ground chile pepper
- 1 teaspoon fresh thyme leaves, or ½ teaspoon dried
- Freshly ground black pepper
- ½ cup of your favorite blue cheese (about ⅓ pound)
- ¼ cup dried unseasoned bread crumbs

TOOLS: *9-inch square or 10 by 7-inch rectangular baking dish*

KITCHEN NOTES: *Look for medium-starch potatoes for melting-est texture; I've used Yellow Finn and Yukon Gold with great success. I do not recommend using skim milk for the Mornay sauce; you need some fat to create voluptuous results. The entire dish can be assembled a few hours in advance and refrigerated until ready to bake and serve. Leftovers are great, gently reheated under a foil tent.*

clear streak on the back of the spoon; I say, keep stirring for another 90 seconds after that clear streak, even if it means stirring off heat. You really do want a thick sauce to ensure maximum gratin gooeyness in the oven. This should take a total of 10 to 11 minutes.

From béchamel to Mornay sauce: Stir in the salt, paprika, thyme, and black pepper. Whisk in the blue cheese until the cheese is completely melted and integrated with the sauce. Taste the sauce for seasonings and adjust accordingly. Remove the sauce from the heat and cover.

Preheat the oven to 350°F.

Assembly: Thoroughly drain the sliced potatoes and turnips of any remaining water. Cover the bottom of the dish with rows of the sliced vegetables, arranged in an overlapping fashion. It doesn't matter if you mix and match, so long as there's even coverage. Cover the layer with a ladleful of sauce, then continue with the next layer and an addition of sauce. You will have a total of three or four layers. Sprinkle the top with the bread crumbs and place the dish on the middle rack of the oven.

Bake for 55 to 60 minutes, or until a paring knife glides effortlessly into the gratin. For a golden top, transfer the gratin to the top rack of the oven and broil for about 60 seconds.

Let the gratin rest and cool for about 10 minutes before cutting and serving.

MAKES 6 TO 8 SERVINGS

CARROT-FENNEL SOUP V GF

- 1 fennel bulb (about ¾ pound)
- 3 tablespoons olive oil
- 1 medium-size onion, chopped roughly (about 1½ cups)
- 2 garlic cloves, peeled and left whole
- 1 pound carrots, scrubbed thoroughly, peeled, and cut into 2-inch pieces (about 5 medium-size carrots)
- 1 (1½-pound) sweet potato or garnet yam, scrubbed thoroughly, peeled, and cut into 2-inch pieces
- 1 teaspoon salt
- 1 teaspoon ground coriander
- ⅛ teaspoon paprika or medium-heat ground chile pepper
- A few whole sprigs of fresh thyme (optional but nice)
- 4 cups water
- 1 teaspoon toasted fennel seeds, for garnish

TOOLS: *Immersion or stand blender or food processor*

I love the idea of carrot soup but am usually disappointed by watery, one-dimensional orange broth. With the addition of fennel, the soup doesn't scream "fennel"; rather, it adds depth of flavor, and the lone sweet potato is there for body. The fennel-seed topper is a really nice surprise and pulls all the flavors together.

HERE'S WHAT YOU DO:

Remove the fronds from the fennel bulb and cut the bulb into slices about ¼-inch thick.

In a large saucepan or soup pot fitted with a lid, heat the oil over medium heat. Add the fennel, onion, and garlic and cook until the fennel and onion are softened, about 5 minutes. Add the carrots and sweet potato and stir until coated by the oil. Stir in the salt, coriander, paprika, and thyme (if using), making sure the seasonings are well distributed.

Pour in the water, which will just cover the vegetables. Increase the heat to medium-high, and bring the mixture to a boil. Lower the heat to low, cover, and simmer until the carrots and sweet potato are fork tender, about 25 minutes.

Meanwhile, place the fennel seeds in a skillet over low-medium heat and toast until slightly golden, about 2 minutes. Shake the skillet to keep from burning. Remove from the heat and reserve for garnish.

Remove the thyme sprigs, then carefully puree the soup (it will be hot!), using an immersion blender, stand blender, or food processor, until smooth and well blended. If pureeing off the stove, return the soup to the heat, taste for seasoning, and adjust accordingly. Heat until warmed through, and serve hot, with a sprinkling of the fennel seeds.

MAKES ABOUT 6 SERVINGS

BROILED GRAPEFRUIT ROUNDS WITH MASSAGED FRISÉE SALAD
V GF

If this dish takes you down Memory Lane, join the club. Broiled grapefruit is a dieter's fad from the '70s, of which my mother was a devotee. She'd slice a grapefruit in half, sprinkle it with brown sugar, and place directly under the broiler for a brûléed crusty top. She'd wriggle the fruit loose with a spoon that had a serrated tip and a long handle. For a twenty-first-century twist on this disco-era classic, I slice the fruit into ½-inch-thick rounds (no retro spoon necessary), topped off with a lemony frisée salad. Breakfast becomes a dinner side, and a very glam one at that.

HERE'S WHAT YOU DO:

Place the frisée in a large bowl and add 2 tablespoons of the lemon juice, 2 tablespoons of the olive oil, and ¼ teaspoon of the salt. With your hands, toss the frisée as if you were massaging it; this not only ensures even coverage of the seasonings but also helps tenderize the raw greens. Taste and add the remaining lemon juice, olive oil, and salt as needed. Allow the greens to sit and marinate for at least 20 minutes.

Meanwhile, prepare the grapefruit: Shallowly slice off one end of the grapefruit so that it has a flat edge. Do not remove the skin from the rest of the fruit. Cut into rounds about ½-inch thick, one per person.

Preheat the oven to the BROIL setting and line a baking sheet with parchment paper.

Arrange the grapefruit in a single layer on the prepared pan. Sprinkle ½ teaspoon of the brown sugar on the top of each grapefruit, so that it's evenly distributed. Place the grapefruit under the broiler for 5 minutes.

Using a ⅓-cup measure, mound the salad atop each broiled grapefruit round. Garnish with almonds, if using.

MAKES 6 SERVINGS

- 3 cups frisée or escarole that has been washed, dried, and chopped finely
- 2 to 3 tablespoons freshly squeezed lemon juice
- 2 to 3 tablespoons olive oil
- ¼ to ½ teaspoon salt
- 2 to 3 Ruby Red grapefruit
- 1 tablespoon light or dark brown sugar
- Optional garnish: ¼ cup unsalted roasted almonds, chopped

CRANBERRY-PISTACHIO BISCOTTI

These twice-baked biscuits have been a mainstay of my holiday cookie repertoire for as long as I've been cooking professionally. The latest version calls for less butter, sugar, and eggs than did my very first batch baked more than fifteen years ago, but the adjustments are undetectable.

- 1 cup granulated sugar
- 6 tablespoons butter, softened slightly and cut into 6 pieces
- 3 eggs
- 2 teaspoons vanilla extract
- 3 cups all-purpose flour
- 1 teaspoon baking powder
- ½ teaspoon salt
- ¾ cup dried cranberries, chopped roughly
- ¾ cup unsalted pistachios, shelled and chopped

TOOLS: *Parchment paper, handheld electric mixer*

HERE'S WHAT YOU DO:

In a large bowl, cream the sugar and butter until light in color and fluffy, 2 to 3 minutes.

In a small bowl, fork-whisk the eggs and measure out 1 tablespoon, reserving for the egg wash. Add the beaten-egg majority to the creamed mixture, plus the vanilla, and mix until blended and increasingly fluffy.

Add the flour, baking powder, and salt to the wet ingredients and mix until just incorporated. Switch to a rubber spatula or wooden spoon, and, by hand, stir in the dried cranberries and pistachios until evenly distributed.

Preheat the oven to 350°F. Have two pieces of parchment paper at the ready, dusted lightly with flour.

Turn out the dough, which will be stiff and sticky, onto one of the parchment sheets. Cut the dough in half. Shape each dough half into a flattened rectangular raft, at least 12 inches long and 2 inches wide, on each parchment sheet. Don't worry if it's not perfect.

Transfer each dough rectangle (and underlying parchment paper) to a baking sheet. With a pastry brush, lightly coat the top with some of the leftover beaten egg.

Bake until half-done, about 25 minutes. Cut each dough rectangle on the diagonal into ½-inch slices. Turn the slices on their side and spread evenly on the baking sheet. Return the cookies to the oven for an additional 15 minutes.

Let the biscotti cool completely on a rack. Stored in an airtight container, the biscotti will keep for a few weeks.

MAKES ABOUT 40 BISCOTTI

CHOCOLATE BARK

Talk about glam! In less than an hour you can make your own chocolate shop–style confections that will have your guests swooning. Melted chocolate meets dried fruit, nuts, and a zippy hit of crystalized ginger, then poured onto a baking tray to set up and mold in the refrigerator. Once it hardens, you can cut the chocolate into neatly pruned twigs or break into free-style driftwood. Whatever you choose, it's a stunning sweet ending. Keep chilled and covered until ready to serve.

HERE'S WHAT YOU DO:

Line a baking sheet with parchment or waxed paper.

Melt the chocolate. You can do this one of two ways, in a microwave oven or in a makeshift double boiler: pour a few inches of water into a medium-size saucepan and place a metal bowl on top that sits snugly yet doesn't touch the water, then add the chocolate and melt over low heat. Remove from the heat and quickly stir in the nuts, dried fruit, crystallized ginger (and sea salt, if using) until well mixed.

Pour the mixture onto the prepared sheet and spread into a rectangle about 12 by 8-inches, making sure that there are no holes or gaps. Refrigerate for about 25 minutes, or until firm enough to cut.

With a serrated knife, cut the bark into strips in the size of your choice. Keep cold until ready to serve. The bark keeps best in an airtight container in the refrigerator for up to 2 weeks.

MAKES AT LEAST 2 DOZEN PIECES

- 8 ounces bittersweet or semisweet chocolate, chopped finely
- ¾ cup unsalted walnut or pecan halves, chopped coarsely
- ¾ cup dried cherries, cranberries or currants, chopped coarsely
- 3 tablespoons crystallized ginger, chopped finely
- ½ teaspoon sel gris or your favorite sea salt (optional)

TOOLS: *Parchment paper or waxed paper*

HANUKKAH: HOT OIL TREATMENT

For eight days in December, Jews celebrate the Festival of Lights, which commemorates the Maccabean victory over the Syrian-Greeks and the resulting reclamation of the temple of Jerusalem. The oft-mentioned "miracle of Hanukkah" refers to the rededicated temple's menorah that stayed alight for eight days on one day's supply of oil. The lasting power of the oil is celebrated with an abundance of fried foods, most notably latkes (a.k.a. potato pancakes). This rendition (from *The Meat Lover's Meatless Cookbook*) boils the potatoes whole before grating, an extra step that creates a starchier result and obviates the need for egg or any binder whatsoever. With a crisp edge and soft, melty center, this pan-size latke looks like a giant hash brown.

Most of the Jews I know can't imagine Hanukkah without latkes, but if you're looking to expand your fried horizons, consider heating some oil for a batch of Spinach Pakoras (page 34), Hush Puppies (page 99), or Chickpea Fries (page 159). Although it doesn't resemble foil-wrapped Hanukkah *gelt*, the fruit-and-nut-studded chocolate bark (page 71) looks and tastes like big money.

FAMILY-STYLE LATKE GF V

HERE'S WHAT YOU DO:

Bring the water and 2 teaspoons of the salt to a boil in a medium-size saucepan fitted with a lid. Add the potatoes, cover, and lower the heat to medium-high. Cook for 22 minutes (the potatoes will only be slightly tender). Meanwhile, have ready a bowl of ice-cold water.

While the potatoes cook, coarsely grate the onion, using a box grater.

Remove the potatoes from the boiling water and transfer to the bowl of cold water. Allow to cool for about 10 minutes. Peel away the skin and coarsely grate the potatoes.

Drain the onion of any residual water and add it to the grated potatoes. Add the remaining ½ teaspoon of salt and black pepper to taste, gently stirring with a rubber spatula.

Have a heatproof cutting board at the ready. Heat a shallow 10-inch skillet over medium-high heat, then add 2 tablespoons of the oil, tilting the skillet for even coverage. Move the skillet off the heat and transfer the potato mixture into the skillet, pressing it evenly until the entire surface is covered with potatoes, looking like a pie, about ¼-inch thick.

Return the skillet to the burner over medium-high heat, or hot enough that the oil sizzles but doesn't burn the latke. Fry the first side for 12 minutes, keeping a close eye on the latke's progress.

Turn off the heat and place the cutting board on top of the skillet. With one hand on top of the cutting board and the other hand on the skillet handle, invert the latke.

Return the skillet to the burner, swirl in the remaining oil over medium-high heat, and carefully slide the latke back into the skillet. Cook the second side for 10 minutes, adjusting the heat as necessary to minimize burning.

Cut the latke into wedges and serve hot with horseradish yogurt "cream" or applesauce (or just all by its savory self).

MAKES 4 SIDE-DISH SERVINGS. FOR A PARTY OF SIX, DOUBLE THE AMOUNTS AND FRY TWO LATKES SIMULTANEOUSLY, OR KEEP ONE WARM IN A 200°F OVEN WHILE THE SECOND LATKE COOKS.

- 5 cups water
- 2 1/2 teaspoons salt
- 12 ounces medium-starch (Yellow Finn or Yukon Gold) or russet potatoes, scrubbed thoroughly
- 1/2 medium-size onion
- Freshly ground black pepper
- 3 tablespoons neutral oil

TOOLS: *10-inch shallow skillet, box grater, heatproof cutting board*

- ½ cup 2% or "traditional" full-fat plain Greek yogurt
- 3 to 4 tablespoons prepared horseradish
- Zest of 1 lemon, chopped
- Salt
- 3 fresh chives, chopped into ringlets, for garnish (optional)

HORSERADISH YOGURT "CREAM"

Instead of the traditional sour cream, I use plain yogurt here, which has plenty of tang, mouthfeel—and protein!

HERE'S WHAT YOU DO:

Place the yogurt in a small bowl and stir vigorously until loosened and somewhat whipped in appearance. Stir in 3 tablespoons of the horseradish; taste and add more as needed. Stir in the lemon zest; taste for salt and add as needed. Sprinkle with the chives, if using.

MAKES ABOUT ¾ CUP YOGURT "CREAM"

APPLESAUCE

(UPDATED FROM *THE MEAT LOVER'S MEATLESS COOKBOOK*)

`GF` `V`

HERE'S WHAT YOU DO:

Peel the apples and thinly slice off their tops and bottoms. Using the core as your focal point, visualize each apple as a four-sided object. Place the blade of your knife on the fleshy edge of the core and slice from top to bottom. You should have four equal pieces, with only the core remaining.

Slice each piece into fourths and place in a medium-size saucepan. Add the lemon juice and water; the apples should be barely covered. Bring to a boil over medium-high heat, then lower the heat and cook at a gentle simmer, allowing the apples to soften, reduce, and thicken into a sauce. This should take no more than 15 minutes.

Stir in the cinnamon, then taste the apples for sweetness and add the sugar as you see fit. The sauce is done when the apples are completely soft and broken up. For a more pureed consistency, use a potato masher or wooden spoon.

Serve warm or let cool and store in the refrigerator in an airtight container for 3 days.

MAKES 4 SERVINGS

- 4 medium-size apples (a mix of Empire, Granny Smith, Jonathan, to name a few, for variety of flavor and texture)
- Juice of ½ lemon
- 1 cup water
- Pinch of ground cinnamon
- ⅛ to ¼ cup granulated sugar (optional)

CHRISTMAS

Christmas is the most global of all holidays, celebrated by Christians and non-believers alike. It is the one holiday that is both religious and secular, cultural and pop-cultural, commercial and traditional.

Maybe you'll make gingerbread men—or reservations for Christmas Day at a Chinese restaurant. You might curl ribbon for packages or curl up in front of the television for an *It's a Wonderful Life* marathon.

For those who celebrate, the traditions are countless and are as varied as the globe, sometimes even within the same family. For many, it's a time to pull out all the stops for "the most wonderful time of the year" and put on a mighty fine spread. To that end, I've curated some of the most festive, party-esque dishes from the collection to help you create your very own Christmas smorgasbord, sit-down affair, or something in between.

RINGING IN THE NEW YEAR

Taking stock. That's what I like to do on the last and first day of the year, and often I see my reflection at the stove. I can't remember the last time I spent New Year's Eve out on the town, and I know it's because the evening was expensive, the food disappointing, and my expectations dashed. Hands down, my most memorable year-ends/beginnings are spent at home, cooking and commemorating the highs and lows of the previous twelve months.

Well before I married a Southerner, black-eyed peas were part of my New Year's ritual, and in this menu, I find a new way to get my dose of hoppin' John good luck—in a paella pan. It is such a festive, bright-eyed presentation, perfect for a crowd. You'll note a few other good-luck traditions getting a nod—lentils, traditionally eaten in Italy at New Year's; and collard greens, representing the "green" of more prosperous days to come. If you're out of time, come back to this menu and say hello to the *stromboli*. It is a mighty festive dish all on its own and perfect for munching in front of the TV while the Rose Bowl parades by.

BLACK-EYED PEA PAELLA 🅥 🄶🄵

- 4 cups vegetable stock (page 214)
- 5 tablespoons olive oil
- 1 cup diced onion (more than ½ medium-size onion)
- 1 cup seeded and diced bell pepper of your favorite color (about 1 medium-size pepper)
- 1 (16-ounce) bag frozen black-eyed peas, or 1 cup dried black-eyed peas, cooked*
- 1½ teaspoons smoked paprika
- 2 cloves garlic, chopped finely
- 1¼ cups tomato puree
- ½ teaspoon crumbled saffron (optional)
- ½ cup white wine you enjoy drinking
- ½ teaspoon salt, plus more to taste
- 2 cups uncooked short-grain white rice (1 pound)
- Optional garnishes: Pickled peppers, chopped fresh parsley, lemon zest

TOOLS: *15-inch paella pan*

*To cook dried black-eyed peas: Soak the peas for at least 2 hours in enough water to cover by at least 2 inches. Drain the peas, then place in a large pot with 4 cups of water. Bring to a lively simmer over medium-high heat. Cook at a hard boil for 5 minutes, then lower the heat, cover, and simmer until the beans are tender to the bite. This should take about 1 hour.

I learned how to make paella many years ago from one of Spain's great culinary ambassadors, chef José Andrés. Using the technique Andrés taught me, I have created a meatless version with black-eyed peas, a new twist on New Year's hoppin' John.

The amounts below are for six hearty servings. Ideally, you'll want to use a 15-inch paella pan to ensure the most even cooking results, but don't worry if that's not an option. Use a wide and shallow skillet (lid not necessary) as close to 15 inches in diameter as you can get. For a half-batch, use a pan about 10 inches wide.

Saffron, which is a spice derived from a variety of crocus, is a traditional seasoning in paella, for both flavor and color. For this dual tribute to the Catalan and the American South, the saffron is not as integral to the final dish as is the *pimentón* (smoked paprika), which adds layers of flavor to the beans. You can do this dish without the saffron, but in my humble opinion, you can't do it without the *pimentón*.

HERE'S WHAT YOU DO:

In a medium-size saucepan, warm the vegetable stock until heated through and keep covered, on low, until ready to use.

Over medium-high heat, heat the paella pan until it's too hot to place your hand about 3 inches above the pan. Add 3 tablespoons of the olive oil, tilting the pan so that the oil coats the entire bottom surface. Lower the heat to medium, add the onion, and cook until slightly softened, about 5 minutes, stirring occasionally to keep from burning or sticking. Add the bell pepper, stir well, and cook for an additional 3 minutes. Add the black-eyed peas and smoked paprika, stirring until the vegetables are evenly coated with the spice, about 90 seconds.

Transfer the black-eyed pea mixture to a bowl and set aside.

Wipe the pan clean with a dry paper towel to remove any burnt, stuck-on bits. Add the remaining olive oil plus the garlic and cook over medium heat until, as chef Andrés says, "they dance." (When heated, the garlic moves around the pan in the bubbling oil.)

Add the tomato puree and stir often, over the next 5 minutes, until the color has transformed from red to a more golden, orange-brown shade. Add the saffron, if using. Then add the white wine and increase the heat to medium-high, stirring to keep from burning.

Return the black-eyed pea mixture to the pan. Add the stock. Bring to a boil, taste for salt, then season accordingly. You want the mixture to be slightly salty. This is also your last chance to add salt before the rice is added.

Add the rice and set a timer for 16 minutes. For the first 6 minutes, gently stir the paella, to minimize burning and sticking. For the remaining cooking time, please heed the advice I learned from chef Andrés: *no more stirring or touching*. Otherwise, you will have a gummy rice concoction. This is also why you cannot add salt at this stage.

At minute 16, taste a grain of rice for doneness. It should be slightly al dente, like risotto. Turn off the heat and allow the paella to sit for at least 5 minutes. The results should be dry, not soupy.

Serve hot in bowls.

MAKES 6 SERVINGS. YOU MAY DOUBLE OR HALVE AMOUNTS, BUT YOU'LL NEED TO USE THE APPROPRIATELY SIZED PAN.

COLLARD DOLMADES `GF` `V`

It's been many years since I learned how to stuff grape leaves like Nada Kattar used to make back in Lebanon. But it is a project, both time-consuming and admittedly tedious, that I'll never forget. I'll never forget because anyone who has ever been gifted with a hand-stuffed and rolled grape leaf knows that it is an act of love. What follows is a meatless version of Nada's filling, with collard greens standing in for the grape leaves. In the American South, collards are traditionally eaten on New Year's Day to usher in good fortune. So in just one little parcel, you get both love and money. I can't think of a more auspicious way to start off a new year. (Nada is mom to my good pal Pierre, who introduced us.)

HERE'S WHAT YOU DO:

Bring the water to a boil in a large saucepan. Parboil the collard greens in small batches (up to five leaves at a time) for 5 minutes. With a pair of tongs, remove the leaves and drain on a wire rack or in a colander. (It's okay to stack them.) Before adding more leaves to the pot, return the water to a boil.

Place the chickpeas in a food processor and pulse three times. You are looking for a slightly chopped result, with plenty of texture. (This can also be done in a mini chopper.)

In a medium-size bowl, combine the rice, tomato paste, spices, olive oil, and chickpeas. Add ½ teaspoon of the salt, stir, and taste the mixture. It should be somewhat salty; if not, add the remaining ¼ teaspoon.

Before trimming and filling the leaves, inspect for holes or tears. Use damaged leaves to line (and completely cover) the bottom of your pot. (No damaged leaves? Set aside the trimmed scraps and a few whole leaves for lining.)

- 8 cups water
- About 3 bunches collard greens, washed thoroughly
- 1 cup cooked chickpeas (if using a 15-ounce can, you will have ½ cup left over for another use)
- 1 cup uncooked short-grain white rice
- 1 tablespoon tomato paste, or 2 fresh plum tomatoes, seeded and diced
- Heaping ¼ teaspoon ground allspice
- Heaping ¼ teaspoon ground cinnamon
- 2 tablespoons olive oil
- 1 cup cooked chickpeas (if using a 15-ounce can, you will have ½ cup left over for another use)
- ½ to ¾ teaspoon salt
- 7 cloves garlic, peeled and left whole
- ¼ cup freshly squeezed lemon juice

TOOLS: *Covered pot at least 9 inches wide, food processor or mini chopper*

Working with the leaves—patted dry—one at a time, place the stem side closest to you, vein side up. With a knife or kitchen shears, cut off the stem where it meets the bottom edge of the leaf. Continue cutting along each side of the middle rib, for at least ½ inch, which will be quite stiff and thick. (You want to be able to bend the leaf.) You'll have leaf flaps on each end.

Measure out 2 teaspoons of filling, one for each side of the rib, and place at the bottom of the leaf, spreading evenly across each side. (For large leaves, add 1 additional teaspoon, for a total of 1 tablespoon of filling.)

Lay the leaf flaps on each side over the filling. Tuck the sides of the leaf in, then roll. Alternate tucking the flaps with rolling. Do not roll too tightly, or the rice will not expand. Seal the parcel by pressing the end with your finger.

Stack the rolls in your leaf-lined pot, in snug rows.

Gradually surround the rolls with water, leaving the top fourth of the leaves exposed. The water amounts will vary depending on the size of the saucepan and the height of the stacked rolls. Scatter the garlic on top. Place a small heatproof salad plate on top of the rolls, cover, and cook over medium-low heat for 15 to 20 minutes.

Remove the plate and pour the lemon juice over the rolls. Add more water if it has exposed more than the top half of the rolls. Return the plate and the lid and cook for an additional 20 minutes. With a paring knife, poke one of the rolls and test the rice for doneness; it should be tender to the bite.

Continue cooking in 10-minute increments until the rice is tender.

With tongs, gently transfer the rolls to a platter. Pour any remaining liquid on top, plus the softened garlic cloves. Serve at room temperature. If making in advance, let cool before refrigerating. Bring to room temperature about an hour before serving.

MAKES ABOUT 36 PIECES

KITCHEN NOTES: *This dish is not difficult, but it does take a few hours due to the time-intensive hand filling and rolling of each collard leaf. The reward for all of your work is about three dozen dolmades that will feed a crowd. They benefit from being cooked a day or two in advance, as they deepen in flavor.*

The listed amounts yield 2 cups of filling. The total number of dolmades filled will vary depending on the size of the leaves and number of leaves per bunch. A typical supermarket bunch contains about ten leaves. You can parboil the collards in advance and wrap them well in plastic until ready to fill.

Lastly, unlike their grape leaf counterparts, collard rolls will not be perfectly symmetrical and as neatly wrapped. Due to their larger size, you may prefer to eat with a fork.

STROMBOLI KIDDO

This recipe is dedicated to Dennis Coyle, a longtime reader and avid cook, who has tested recipes for both Meat Lover's Meatless collections. Dennis has the great gift of kitchen improv, as he's always writing me of his adventures putting his own spin on my recipes. One such adventure included my pizza dough (from *The Meat Lover's Meatless Cookbook*) shaped into a rectangle, filled and rolled up into a stromboli, just like the old-time pizza shops in Philadelphia, where I grew up. Dennis will notice that his beloved pepperoni and sausage is absent from this version, but I reckon he'll find it passes muster, especially for a mixed-crowd party.

HERE'S WHAT YOU DO:

Heat the water to 100°F (this is very warm but far from boiling) and pour into a small bowl. Sprinkle the yeast, sugar, and 1 tablespoon of the flour over the water. With a fork, stir until dissolved, then cover the bowl and allow the mixture to sit at room temperature until it is slightly foamy, about 15 minutes.

In a large bowl (think wide and shallow versus tall and narrow), place 1 cup of the flour, the salt, and the olive oil and stir with a rubber spatula or wooden spoon. Add the yeast mixture and stir until just mixed. Add the remaining flour, ½ cup at a time, stirring between flour additions. You are looking for a soft, sticky dough that is just pulling away from the sides of the bowl. Depending on the weather (humidity, heat), the total amount of flour used will vary between 2½ and 3½ cups. It's unnecessary to use the maximum amount.

Lightly dust a work surface with flour and turn the dough out of the bowl onto the work surface.

Begin kneading the dough in the following manner: Punch gently but firmly, fold in half, and turn (rotate 15 minutes on your imaginary clock, or one-quarter turn). For the next 6 minutes, or until your dough becomes a smooth, soft, springy ball, your mantra is *punch, fold, turn.*

▶ ▶ ▶

DOUGH:

- 1 cup water
- 1 (¼-ounce) envelope active dry yeast, or 2¼ teaspoons from a jar
- Pinch of sugar
- About 3 cups all-purpose flour
- 1 teaspoon salt
- 1 tablespoon olive oil

KITCHEN NOTES: *There are countless ways to jazz up a stromboli roll, which is an open invitation to get creative and to use what's in the pantry. That said, there are a few important things to keep in mind: No matter which fixin's you decide on, make sure they're not too saucy or wet, which will yield very leaky and soggy results. (That means no marinara sauce, at least not on the inside).*

As tempting as it is, you also don't want to load up your stromboli with everything but the kitchen sink. Weighed down, the dough is susceptible to tearing; it also results in messy serving slices and unevenly cooked dough. Use the following ingredients and amounts as a guide, then go wild.

If, like Dennis, you're craving marinara sauce for dipping, that can be warmed up while the stromboli is baking. Details are on page 92.

STROMBOLI FILLING TEMPLATE:

- 1 teaspoon dried oregano
- ⅓ cup pesto (the Kale Pesto on page 52 works great), olive tapenade, or sun-dried tomato spread
- ⅓ cup roasted or pickled peppers or drained artichoke hearts
- ¼ cup grated Parmigiano-Reggiano or pecorino cheese
- 1 cup spinach, arugula, or chard that has been washed, dried, and chopped, then seasoned with 1 tablespoon of olive oil and salt to taste
- ½ to ¾ cup grated mozzarella or provolone cheese, to taste

TOOLS: *Parchment paper or silicone baking mat*

Lightly oil a large bowl and place the dough in the bowl, turning to coat. Cover the bowl with a towel or plastic wrap. (Alternatively, place the dough in a lightly greased pot with a lid.) Place in a warm spot, away from drafts. Let rise until doubled, about 1 hour.

At this point, the risen dough may be wrapped in plastic and refrigerated (or frozen) for later use. (Thaw the frozen dough in the refrigerator and allow the chilled dough to come to room temperature for at least 15 minutes before rolling and shaping.)

Meanwhile, prepare the filling (details follow).

Stromboli Filling Template

HERE'S WHAT YOU DO:

Preheat the oven to 375°F.

On parchment paper or a silicone mat, roll or shape the dough into a 10 by 14-inch rectangle that is about ½-inch thick. Have a wee bit of flour on hand in case dough sticks to your work surface.

Work with the long side of the dough rectangle closest to you. Sprinkle the oregano evenly over the dough.

Use the ingredient list as a guide and work in the suggested order. Apply the filling to the two-thirds of the dough closest to you, keeping 1-inch dough borders free of any filling. If you need a visual reminder, make indentations with a paring knife.

Roll the dough away from you, jelly-roll style, into a log, making sure that the seam and the ends are sealed, with the seam on the bottom.

Holding the parchment paper or baking mat by the ends, carefully transport the dough log to a baking sheet. If the *stromboli* is too long, feel free to arrange it into a horseshoe or snake shape. With a paring knife, make a few slashes on the top of the dough. For a deeper color, you may brush the dough with olive oil.

Bake until the dough is golden and makes a hollow sound when you tap the exterior, about 30 minutes. Remove from the oven and allow to cool for 5 minutes. Slice into wedges and eat hot or at room temperature.

MAKES ABOUT 12 PIECES

SWEET POTATO HUMMUS

- 2 pounds orange-fleshed sweet potatoes (also sold as garnet or jewel yams)
- 1 medium-size yellow onion
- Olive oil, for brushing
- 1 clove garlic, minced
- 2 tablespoons tahini
- ¼ teaspoon paprika or other medium-heat ground chile pepper
- ½ teaspoon salt
- 2 to 3 tablespoons freshly squeezed lemon juice (about ½ medium-size lemon)

TOOLS: *Food processor or heavy-duty stand blender*

Given that *hummus* is derived from the Arabic word for "chickpeas," this is a loose interpretation of the beloved Middle Eastern spread, but a fun way to get your daily dose of vitamin A and antioxidants. Kids go crazy for this stuff; make a batch for the next birthday party and watch it disappear.

HERE'S WHAT YOU DO:

Preheat the oven to 400°F.

Wash and scrub the sweet potatoes. Cut into 3- to 4-inch pieces, regardless of the width. Keep the skins on.

Slice the onion in half and peel. Brush the onion and sweet potatoes with olive oil and place in a baking dish in a single layer. Cover with foil and roast for 1 hour; the sweet potatoes should be extremely tender.

Let cool for about 10 minutes. Peel off the skins of the sweet potatoes.

Place all the roasted vegetables in the bowl of a food processor or heavy-duty stand blender and puree. Add the garlic, tahini, paprika, and salt and blend. Then gradually add 2 tablespoons of the lemon juice and taste. Add more as needed.

Serve at room temperature with chopped fruits and vegetables: apples, bell peppers, celery, endive, jicama, and pears are all great dipping companions.

Keeps well in an airtight container in the refrigerator for at least 3 days. The garlic flavor deepens with time.

MAKES 2½ CUPS HUMMUS

LENTIL PÂTÉ `GF`

This little number is inspired by chicken liver terrine, a French brasserie and Jewish delicatessen classic. Replicating the same technique and flavor notes from a passed-down recipe, I swap out the livers with legumes. I won't say you can trick your chicken liver–loving pals, but you will astonish them.

HERE'S WHAT YOU DO:

Place the lentils, water, and garlic in a medium-size saucepan. The water should be about 2 inches above the lentils. Add more as needed. Over medium-high heat, bring the mixture to a boil. Lower the heat to medium-low and cook at a simmer until tender to the bite, 30 to 35 minutes. Season with ½ teaspoon of the salt.

While the lentils cook, melt the butter in a 9- or 10-inch skillet over medium-high heat. Add the shallot, stir to coat with the butter, and cook until thick, jamlike, and caramelized, 20 to 25 minutes. Lower the heat if the shallot begins to char. Increase the heat and add the booze (or apple cider), allowing it to evaporate, 2 to 3 minutes. Stir in the rosemary, nutmeg, and the remaining ¼ teaspoon of the salt, then turn off the heat.

Drain the lentils and transfer to a baking sheet to cool in a single layer for 10 minutes. Make sure you bring along the cooked garlic.

Transfer the shallot mixture to the bowl of a food processor or stand blender and blend, scraping the sides of the bowl as necessary. Add the lentils and garlic, and blend until you have a creamy mixture with as few lumps as possible.

Season with the black pepper to taste (and more salt if needed), and scoop into a 4-inch ramekin or four-edged dish.

(The spread looks more pâtélike in a shaped dish than freestyle in a cereal bowl.) Place in the refrigerator for at least 45 minutes; the pâté deepens in flavor when slightly chilled.

Serve with toast points or baguette slices, or with carrot, celery, or jicama sticks, or endive leaves.

MAKES A LITTLE OVER 2 CUPS PÂTÉ

- 1 cup dried brown or green lentils
- 3 cups water
- 2 cloves garlic, peeled and left whole
- ½ to ¾ teaspoon salt, plus more to taste
- 4 tablespoons butter
- 1 cup peeled and thinly sliced shallot (about 4 bulbs)
- ¼ cup bourbon or cognac (booze-free option: apple cider)
- 2 teaspoons chopped fresh rosemary (from at least 2 sprigs)
- ½ teaspoon grated nutmeg
- Freshly ground black pepper

TOOLS: *Food processor or stand blender*

BLOOD ORANGE FILLING:

- 4 to 6 medium-size blood oranges
- 1 teaspoon ground cinnamon
- 1 tablespoon all-purpose flour or cornstarch
- ½ cup granulated sugar, plus more to taste
- Pinch of salt

ENLIGHTENED PIE DOUGH:

- 4 tablespoons olive oil
- ½ cup water
- 2 cups all-purpose flour, at room temperature, plus more for dusting
- ¼ teaspoon salt
- ¼ teaspoon baking powder
- 4 tablespoons butter, cut into tablespoon-size pieces
- 2 to 3 tablespoons apricot or raspberry jam
- Egg white wash: 1 egg white, beaten with 1 tablespoon water
- 1 to 2 tablespoons granulated or coarse sugar

TOOLS: *Food processor, 5-inch dough scraper, silicone baking mat or parchment paper, silicone or pastry brush*

BLOOD ORANGE GALETTE

This is the galette version of the butter–olive oil Enlightened Pie Dough described in the Thanksgiving and Fourth of July menus (pages 43 and 188), with adjusted amounts for a smaller, free-form tart. If you've never made a galette, it's more rustic both in presentation and sometimes texture. I often like to describe it as a big Pop-Tart.

HERE'S WHAT YOU DO:

Blood Orange Filling

With a paring knife, remove the peel and pith of the blood oranges. Begin by slicing off the peel of both ends so that the fruit can sit upright. From top to bottom, slice away the peel and as much pith as possible without cutting into the fruit. Trim the pith as needed. Cut the oranges into ¼-inch rounds.

With the tip of the knife, carefully remove any seeds and poke out any remaining white pith knobs in the center of the rounds.

Place the fruit in a medium-size bowl and add the cinnamon, flour, sugar, and salt, stirring gently until completely coated. Allow to macerate for about 30 minutes.

Enlightened Pie Dough

Place the olive oil in a small bowl and set aside.

Place the water in a small saucepan and heat until very hot. It need not be boiling but should be pretty close.

While the water is heating, measure out the flour. Remove 1 tablespoon and reserve for rolling out the dough. (You may need a little bit more than your reserve for a second rolling.) Place in a food processor, along with the salt and the baking powder, and pulse a few times just to mix.

Add the butter. Pulse until the mixture looks and feels like fluffy sand. You should not be able to see butter clumps.

Measure out ¼ cup (4 tablespoons) of the water and add to the oil. With a fork, whisk together; it will look like a vinaigrette.

Pour the oil mixture on top of the flour mixture, and pulse until the dough just comes together. It may slightly pull away from the sides of the bowl. The dough should feel soft, warm, and pliable, not hard and crumbly. If the dough looks as if it needs more liquid, add the hot water in 1-tablespoon increments, pulse, and check the softness of the dough.

Lightly dust your rolling surface with some of the reserved flour, and place the dough on top. Surround the dough with both hands to let it know you're there, or as Kate McDermott says, "give it a good hand-shake," molding it into a cohesive lump.

Roll the dough in quick, even strokes, making a quarter-turn after every few strokes. As you rotate and roll the dough, check regularly to make sure the dough is not sticking. (A dough scraper is helpful at this stage.) The immediate goal is to make a rectangle roughly 9 by 11-inches. (Don't worry if it's not exact.)

Fold the dough like a letter: Starting from a short edge, fold over a third of your dough. Take the opposite edge and fold it to the middle, covering the first fold.

Make a quarter-turn, then roll out the dough into a new rectangle, dusting with flour as needed. Make another letter fold with the dough.

Give the dough another quarter-turn, and roll the dough in all four directions—north, south, east, west. Fold the dough in half into a 4- to 5-inch square packet. Roll lightly on top to seal the layers and surround the edges with both hands to tidy the dough.

Wrap the dough in plastic and allow to rest in the refrigerator for a brief 10 minutes. Unlike an all-butter dough, this dough never goes into a deep sleep and gets cold; think of it as a brief catnap after all that rolling and folding.

Preheat the oven to 425°F.

In a microwave oven or a small saucepan, heat up the jam until melty, like a sauce.

Roll out the dough on the rolling surface. Dust both the top and bottom of the dough with extra flour, as needed. With more of those deft, even strokes, roll the dough into a 9- or 10-inch circle or rectangle.

Brush the surface of the dough with a thin layer of the melted jam, leaving a 2-inch border all around.

▶ ▶ ▶

KITCHEN NOTES: *It's always a good idea to read a recipe in entirety before cooking, but in this case, it's particularly crucial. Playing with dough requires a bit of organization. Make the filling first. You want it to be ready because the dough, once rolled out, waits for no one.*

Blood oranges, which are typically in season from December through March, vary in size. You're looking for a total of 2 cups of fruit for the filling. Don't worry if your total amount of fruit falls short; you can get away with 1¾ cups of filling.

Because a galette is baked free-form without a pan, it's important to shape and roll out dough on a silicone baking mat or parchment paper that will ultimately be transferred to a baking sheet.

Strain the fruit before placing on top of the dough. Arrange the fruit in overlapping fashion, again within the 2-inch border.

With the help of a dough scraper (or the surface underneath), lift the margins of the dough, section by section, over the filling, pressing dough edges when they meet. As much as one-third of the filling in the center will be exposed; that's okay.

Brush the top of the dough with the egg white wash, then sprinkle lightly with the sugar. Brush the exposed fruit with the remaining melted jam.

Transfer the galette (and its liner underneath) to a baking sheet and into the refrigerator for a quick 5-minute chill.

Bake for 5 minutes. Lower the heat to 375°F and bake for an additional 35 to 40 minutes, checking at minute 30 for doneness. The galette is done when the crust is golden and the fruit is bubbling.

Grab the two ends of the parchment or baking mat and transfer the galette to a rack, allowing to cool for about 1 hour.

MAKES 6 TO 8 SERVINGS

THE BIG GAME

Otherwise known as Men in Tights Day, in KOD land. I don't know a touchdown from an offsides, but I do something about television marathon–worthy chow. This year, we're gonna let go of the chicken wings; I promise it won't hurt. The plan I've cooked up isn't just leaner on the jeans; it's downright lip-smacking. The meatball sub—made from lentils—has the all the flavor notes of an old-school Italian-American meatball. Tuck it into a bun with some marinara sauce, and you've got a champion in your own two hands. Lest you think the quinoa brownies are for the bake sale set, one bite and you'll be wondering where they've been all your life. P.S. This could do delicious double duty during NCAA's tournament known as "March Madness."

LENTIL "MEATBALL" SUB
WITH MARINARA `KIDDO`

It started as a daydream. There's a guy, let's call him Luigi, hovering over a cast-iron skillet, delicately turning golf ball–size *polpettine*, the Italian approximation of meat balls, with Dean Martin's "That's Amore" playing on the radio. He's just poured himself a glass of Valpolicella. My mind's eye zooms in on the scene, and I notice that these little brown morsels happily dancing in olive oil are not the stuff of pork or veal—but of lentils. I watch how they get golden and even a little crispy. Luigi ladles some tomato "gravy" into a bowl, then he places a few balls on top. The only thing that's missing is a red checkered tablecloth.

HERE'S WHAT YOU DO:

Cook the rice: Bring ¾ cup of the water to a boil, then add the rice. Return to a boil, lower the heat to a simmer, cover, and cook until the water is absorbed and the rice is tender, 40 to 45 minutes. Off the heat, keep the rice covered for 5 minutes. Measure out ½ cup of the cooked rice and transfer to a baking sheet or plate to cool completely. Refrigerate the remaining 1 cup of rice for another use.

While the rice is cooking, prepare the lentils: Place the lentils in a large saucepan, along with the 2 whole garlic cloves and the remaining 6 cups of the water. Over high heat, bring to a boil, then lower the heat to medium. Cook the lentils until tender, 30 to 35 minutes. Drain thoroughly so that the lentils are dry. Allow to cool completely.

While the lentils cook, prepare the marinara sauce: In a medium-size saucepan, heat 2 tablespoons of the olive oil over medium heat, then add ¼ cup of the onion and the 3 minced garlic cloves, cooking until slightly softened, about 3 minutes. Add 1 teaspoon of the dried oregano and stir occasionally to minimize sticking.

Add the tomato puree and stir to combine the mixture. Bring to a boil, then lower the heat so the sauce can simmer. Cover and cook for about 20 minutes. Keep warm until ready to serve. (For prepared marinara

▶ ▶ ▶

Ingredients

- 6¾ cups water
- ½ cup uncooked medium- or long-grain brown rice
- 1 cup dried brown or green lentils
- 5 garlic cloves: 2 whole, 3 minced
- 2 tablespoons olive oil, plus ½ cup for panfrying
- ¾ cup onion that has been very finely minced or grated using a box grater (about 1 medium-size onion)
- 3 teaspoons dried oregano
- 1 (23- to 28-ounce) container tomato puree
- ½ cup finely grated Parmigiano-Reggiano cheese (or pecorino for a sheep's milk option)
- 1 teaspoon salt
- ½ teaspoon freshly ground black pepper
- ¼ cup unseasoned medium-grind bread crumbs (panko makes a fun textural option)
- 1 egg, beaten lightly
- 6 (6-inch) sub rolls, toasted
- Optional topping: 4 ounces sharp provolone or Cheddar cheese

TOOLS: *Food processor or handheld potato masher, 10- or 12-inch skillet*

KITCHEN NOTES: *Both the lentils and rice must be completely cooled before mixing together and shaping into balls; otherwise you'll have a goopy, unworkable mess on your hands. You'll need about an hour of advance prep time before the meatball assembly can commence. The balls can be assembled in advance and cooked when ready to serve, as can the sauce. The recipe yields 26 to 30 meatballs, which make 6 to 8 ample servings. It is important to note that the balls are more delicate compared to their meaty counterparts, and care should be given when frying.*

Don't sweat it if you're not in the mood to make your own marinara. Should you choose something off the supermarket shelf, choose a brand with as little sugar, salt, and fillers as possible.

Try these in a bowl for a sit-down supper or as a "meatball sub," perfect chow for watching men in tights on television. For a cheesy topper, I recommend having some sharp provolone or Cheddar on hand.

sauce, heat until warmed through over medium heat, cover, and keep warm on low heat.)

Place the cooled lentils and garlic in the bowl of a food processor and pulse until the lentils are mashed. (No food processor? Use a handheld potato masher.) Transfer the mixture to a large mixing bowl, then add the cooled rice, the remaining ½ cup of onion, the remaining 2 teaspoons of oregano, and the grated cheese, salt, black pepper, bread crumbs, and egg.

With a wooden spoon or rubber spatula, stir the mixture until well mixed.

Using a ⅛-cup measure, shape into balls. They will be slightly sticky to the touch. Refrigerate for 20 minutes.

Preheat the oven to 325°F.

Over medium-high heat, heat ¼ cup of the olive oil in a 10- or 12-inch skillet until the oil shimmers. Gently lower the balls into the hot oil, cooking in batches and making sure not to crowd the pan, as they are somewhat delicate and benefit from space. Lower the heat to medium and panfry on first side for about 3 minutes. Turn (or gently nudge) to second side and cook for 2 minutes.

Transfer the first batch to a baking sheet. Add the remaining ¼ cup of olive oil to the skillet for subsequent batches and cook in the same manner. Transfer the balls to the oven to finish cooking, about 5 minutes; the balls will still be somewhat soft to the touch but will have dried out a bit and will have a slightly crispy coating.

To keep the balls warm while you prepare the broccoli rabe, lower the oven temperature to 225°F.

SAUTÉED BROCCOLI RABE   GF V

HERE'S WHAT YOU DO:

Bring the water to a boil in a medium-size saucepan. Add the salt. Add the greens and cook for about 90 seconds. With tongs, remove from the pot and drain in a colander. Pat dry with a towel, then chop into 1-inch pieces.

Swirl the oil into a 10- or 12-inch skillet over medium-high heat, until the oil shimmers. Add the broccoli rabe and garlic, and lower heat to medium to minimize burning the garlic. Cook for about 3 minutes, turning with tongs for even coverage. Season with the red chile pepper flakes, plus salt to taste.

MEAL ASSEMBLY:

In a bowl: Ladle about ½ cup of marinara sauce over three or four lentil balls. Top off each bowl with wilted greens.

As part of a sandwich: Into each toasted sub roll, tuck three or four lentil balls, followed by a minimum of ¼ cup marinara sauce. With tongs, lay about ¼ cup of broccoli rabe on top. For the sharp cheese option, cut into thin slices and lay on top of the sandwich as is or melted under a broiler.

MAKES 6 SERVINGS

- 4 cups water
- 1 teaspoon salt, plus more to taste
- 1 bunch broccoli rabe, washed and stalk ends removed
- 2 tablespoons olive oil
- 1 to 2 cloves garlic, smashed
- ¼ teaspoon red chile pepper flakes

TOOLS: *10- or 12-inch skillet*

KITCHEN NOTES: *Broccoli rabe (also spelled raab) is a cool-weather crop also sold as rapini, choi sum, or Chinese flowering cabbage. It is not the same thing as broccolini, which is much sweeter and more floret-heavy. In fact, it's more closely related to turnip greens than to broccoli. If the assertive-flavored rabe is too bitter for you or it's not available, feel free to substitute other quick-wilting greens, such as chard, spinach, or baby kale. (No need to blanch; just go straight to the sauté step.)*

LIGHTENED-UP OLD-SCHOOL ONION DIP

- 2 tablespoons neutral oil
- 1 large onion, halved and sliced thinly (about 3 cups)
- ½ teaspoon salt, plus more to taste
- Freshly ground black pepper
- 16 ounces "traditional" or 2% plain Greek yogurt
- 1 teaspoon garlic powder
- ½ teaspoon celery seeds
- ½ teaspoon dry mustard
- ¼ to ½ teaspoon ground cumin
- 1 teaspoon Worcestershire sauce (Anchovy-free Plan B: Pickapeppa sauce or ½ teaspoon soy sauce plus ½ teaspoon molasses)
- Dipping vegetable options: Bell pepper, carrots, celery, cucumber, and jicama, cut into handheld-size slices

TOOLS: *10- or 12-inch cast-iron (or equally heavy) skillet, food processor*

KITCHEN NOTES: *Greek yogurt, which is becoming increasingly available in conventional supermarkets, is super creamy and my preference here. If it's just not available in your neck of the woods, don't fret; place a metal sieve over a bowl and pour plain yogurt into the sieve, letting it drain for 30 minutes or so. Although not a deal breaker, the nonfat version is less creamy than its 2% or fuller-fat "traditional" counterparts.*

I can still see the envelope of onion soup mix that my mother would sprinkle over sour cream, pour into a pretty little bowl, and serve with waffle-style potato chips for her bridge club gals. That memory is etched right around 1975. You, too?

As much as I love an occasional dip-and-chip indulgence, the formula of yesteryear inevitably has me scrambling for a pitcher of water (those seasoning packets can be extraordinarily salty and contain a slew of preservatives better left alone). Enter: a spice blend with stuff from the cupboard (and not the lab) and a mess of caramelized onions doing some magic on Greek yogurt (the lightened-up piece of this recipe).

HERE'S WHAT YOU DO:

Over medium-high heat, heat the oil in a 10- or 12-inch cast-iron (or equally heavy) skillet and add the onion slices. Using tongs, turn the onion to coat with the oil. Lower the heat to low and cook, stirring regularly, until the onion is jamlike and caramelized, about 45 minutes. Be careful not to burn.

Season with the salt and pepper to taste and transfer the onion jam to a small bowl. Cover and place in the freezer for 20 minutes.

Transfer the chilled onion jam to the bowl of a food processor and puree. Add the remaining ingredients and blend until smooth.

Serve with your favorite raw vegetables: carrots, celery, bell pepper, cucumber, and jicama are all fun dipping partners.

The flavors mellow and deepen with time. The dip keeps for 3 days in an airtight container in the refrigerator.

MAKES A SCANT 3 CUPS DIP

QUINOA-WALNUT BROWNIES

 GF KIDDO

Cakey this brownie is not; it's fudgy-wudgy all the way. It also happens to be gluten-free: the flour stand-in is quinoa ground in an electric coffee grinder. The slight graininess doesn't distract; rather, it teams up with the chopped walnuts to create a toothsome texture. They are, if I may say so, the cat's pajamas.

HERE'S WHAT YOU DO:

Grease a baking pan and line with parchment paper with a few inches of overhang so you can easily remove brownies after baking. Grind the quinoa in a coffee or spice grinder until it looks powdery, like flour. Transfer to a small bowl and add the salt and the baking powder.

Pour a few inches of water into a medium-size saucepan and place a metal bowl that fits snugly on top, yet without touching the water, to make a double boiler. Place all of the chocolate and the butter in the bowl and melt over medium-low heat. As the mixture melts, the chocolate will take on a glossy sheen. With a heatproof rubber spatula, gently scrape the sides of the bowl and stir. When the mixture is completely melted, it will be shiny and smooth.

Preheat the oven to 325°F.

Remove the bowl from the heat and whisk in the sugar and vanilla, followed by the eggs, one at a time. Switch to a wooden spoon or rubber stirring spatula, and stir in the quinoa mixture until well incorporated. Stir in the walnuts until evenly distributed. Scoop the batter into the prepared pan and place on a baking sheet.

Bake on the middle rack for 35 minutes, or until a skewer inserted into the middle comes out with a small amount of residue. You are looking for a fudgy crumb and overbaking will yield a dry result.

Transfer the pan to a rack and allow to cool completely, at least 1 hour. Using the parchment overhang, remove the brownies from the pan and transfer to a cutting board. Remove the parchment. If the brownies are still even a little bit warm, expect some breakage. Slice and serve.

The brownies freeze well wrapped in foil.

MAKES ABOUT 16 SERVINGS

- ½ cup quinoa, or ⅔ cup quinoa flour
- ½ teaspoon salt
- ½ teaspoon baking powder
- 2 ounces unsweetened chocolate, chopped roughly
- 4 ounces bittersweet chocolate, chopped roughly
- 6 tablespoons butter, cut into 6 pieces
- 1 cup granulated sugar
- 2 teaspoons vanilla extract
- 2 eggs, beaten lightly
- ½ cup unsalted walnuts, chopped roughly

TOOLS: *Electric coffee or spice grinder, parchment paper, balloon whisk, 8- or 9-inch square baking pan*

KITCHEN NOTES: *Quinoa comes in shades of beige, red, and black, and a mélange of all three, sold as "rainbow quinoa." They work equally well, but the beige yields the finest, powdery texture of all. Use what is available. For these brownies use quinoa that's been rinsed before packaging. Ancient Harvest, Bob's Red Mill, Earthly Delights, and Eden Foods all sell rinsed quinoa, as stated on their labels.*

MARDI GRAS

For those who observe Lent, Mardi Gras (also known as Fat Tuesday) is the last night to let it all hang out for forty days. It can also be a time to appreciate the culinary heritage of New Orleans, where Africa meets France meets the bayou. While under French rule in the late 1700s, New Orleans was a hub for pre-Lenten galas.

For this menu, I zoomed in on some of my favorites from the Creole pantry, the dishes you could find in nearly any restaurant in the Big Easy—red beans and rice, bread pudding, blackened catfish. With very little effort, I was able to put an entirely vegan spin on these Creole classics, which speaks to the heat and flavor complexity of a cuisine that is unlike anything else in the world.

The tofu is prepared just as if you had some redfish fillets. The texture is astonishingly similar. I'm confident this menu will make you wanna dance all night. Now where's Trombone Shorty when I need him?

HUSH PUPPIES `GF` `KIDDO`

Traditionally, hush puppies are served with fried fish in the American South, but they pair beautifully with the red beans and rice and the Cajun blackened tofu, which reminds me of blackened catfish.

I also break with buttermilk tradition and try something equally rich—coconut milk—for a nondairy change of pace. You can use the unsweetened variety sold in cans or the newly available fortified kind sold in refrigerated cartons and shelf-stable boxes, as detailed on page (11). To keep tabs on the frying oil temperature, have a candy thermometer on hand. P.S. These can be addictive!

HERE'S WHAT YOU DO:

Place the cornmeal, baking powder, salt, and chile pepper in a medium-size bowl and stir together. Add the scallions, onion, egg, and coconut milk, and stir until well mixed. The mixture will look like wet sand.

Place the oil in a 9-inch-wide deep pot or saucepan and heat until it reaches 350°F.

Arrange a few paper towels on the adjacent work surface to drain the hush puppies after they've been fried.

Using a tablespoon or ice-cream scoop, drop the batter into the hot oil. You should be able to get three to four hush puppies going at the same time. Fry until golden brown and firm on each side, about 60 seconds. Remove with a slotted spoon and transfer to paper towels to drain.

Before adding more batter, remove any burnt bits with the slotted spoon and return the oil to 350°F.

Eat hot or keep warm in the oven at 225°F.

MAKES 20 TO 22 HUSH PUPPIES

- 2 cups medium-grind cornmeal (stone-ground if possible)
- 1 teaspoon baking powder
- 1 teaspoon salt
- ¼ teaspoon ground chile pepper of choice
- ¼ cup scallions, root and dark green tops removed, minced
- ¼ cup very finely minced onion
- 1 egg, beaten lightly
- 1½ cups coconut milk
- 2 cups neutral oil

TOOLS: *Candy thermometer, slotted spoon*

RED BEANS AND (BROWN) RICE
V **GF**

- 1½ cups uncooked medium- or long-grain brown rice
- 2⅔ cups water
- 4 tablespoons neutral oil
- 2 cups diced onion (1 medium-large onion)
- 1 cup diced celery (about 3 stalks)
- 1½ cups seeded and diced bell pepper of any color (1 large)
- 4 cloves garlic, minced
- 1 teaspoon ground chipotle chile pepper
- ¼ to ½ teaspoon cayenne, to taste
- 1½ teaspoons dried oregano
- ½ to 1 teaspoon salt
- 3¾ cups cooked red kidney beans, drained (from three 15-ounce cans or 1½ cups dried beans)
- 1½ cups (12 ounces) lager or other mild-flavored beer (nonalcoholic or gluten-free beer works great) or vegetable stock (page 214)
- 4 scallions, roots and dark green tops removed, sliced into thin rounds, for garnish

TOOLS: *Handheld potato masher*

KITCHEN NOTES: *As part of my ongoing efforts to eat more whole grains, I've swapped out the white rice for brown. If you can't be bothered, go ahead and make a pot of white rice.*

If you've ever been in New Orleans on a Monday, you know that red beans and rice is what's for supper. Traditionally, the dish would be seasoned with leftovers from Sunday dinner, maybe a ham bone or bacon grease. Here, it's all about the plants but no less delicious.

HERE'S WHAT YOU DO:

Bring the rice and the water to a boil in a medium-size saucepan. Cover and cook over low heat until the water is absorbed and the rice is tender to the bite, 40 to 42 minutes.

Keep covered off the heat for 5 minutes, or until ready to serve.

Meanwhile, prepare the beans: In a large soup pot fitted with a lid, heat the oil over medium-high heat. Add the onion, lower the heat to medium, and cook until slightly softened, about 5 minutes. Add the celery and bell pepper, stirring regularly to keep the vegetables from burning. Cook for an additional 4 to 5 minutes, then add the garlic, stir, and cook for an additional 1 to 2 minutes.

Add the chile pepper, cayenne, oregano, and ½ teaspoon of the salt. (Depending on how salty your canned beans are, you may want to start with ¼ teaspoon of salt and add accordingly.) Stir to coat the spices with the vegetables. Add the beans, stir, and add your cooking liquid.

Bring the beans to a boil, then lower the heat, cover, and simmer over medium-low heat, about 20 minutes. Using a ladle, transfer 1½ cups of the beans to a bowl, and mash the beans with a potato masher. Return to the pot and stir; you'll notice a nice thickening under way. Taste for salt, and add the remaining ½ teaspoon if needed. You may continue to simmer the beans for an additional 10 minutes, or serve immediately. Serve with the rice and a sprinkling of the chopped scallions.

Serve with the Cajun Blackened Tofu. Reheats beautifully.

MAKES ABOUT 8 SERVINGS

Soaking and Cooking the Dried Red Beans

Place the beans in a bowl and add enough water to cover by a few inches. Soak for at least 4 hours. (In warmer climes, soak the beans in the refrigerator to avoid sprouting or fermentation.) Drain the beans of the soaking water; you now have about 3¾ cups of soaked beans.

Transfer the beans to a large pot fitted with a lid and add 8 cups of fresh water, which is about 2 inches above the beans, along with the garlic. With the lid on, bring the water to a boil. Remove the lid and cook the beans at a hard boil for 5 minutes. Cover, lower the heat to low, and cook at a gentle simmer. At minute 20, stir in the salt. At minute 45, check the beans for doneness. Cook in 10-minute increments until the beans are tender to the bite, keeping in mind that cooking times may vary, depending on the age of the beans.

Drain the beans in preparation for the next step of the dish. You may reserve the cooking liquid and use as part of the beans and rice.

SOAKING AND COOKING THE DRIED RED BEANS:

- 1½ cups dried red kidney beans
- 2 cloves garlic, peeled and left whole
- ¾ teaspoon salt

KITCHEN NOTES: *I've done this dish with both canned and dried kidney beans that are cooked in advance. They perform equally well. If using canned beans, choose brands with little or no sodium, and if possible, BPA-free cans (see Pantry section on page 7 for details). Details for soaking and cooking the dried beans follow, after the recipe.*

Active cooking time for stewing the beans takes about 35 minutes, just a few minutes shy of the rice, which takes about 40 minutes.

CAJUN BLACKENED TOFU GF V

While in cooking school, I learned how to blacken redfish the old-fashioned way—in a dry, smoking-hot cast-iron skillet—a method popularized in the 1980s by Louisiana chef Paul Prudhomme. When drained of its water and cut into triangles, blackened tofu has a texture reminiscent of chef Paul's famous fish fillets.

HERE'S WHAT YOU DO:

Drain the tofu: Remove from the packages and place each rectangular block on a separate plate. Place a second plate on top and weigh the tofu down with something heavy, such as a can of tomatoes. Allow to sit for about 20 minutes. Drain off the water.

Meanwhile, place the spices and salt in a small bowl and thoroughly mix. Spread the spice blend evenly in the center of a dinner plate.

Working with one tofu block at a time, lay flat on a cutting surface. Cut the tofu block in half on the diagonal so you have two large triangles. Lay each triangle half on its longest side, and from the top short edge, cut into four triangles, ¼ to ½ inch thick.

Brush the tofu with the oil on both sides, then dredge in the spice rub until well coated. Transfer to a baking sheet.

Preheat the oven to 300°F.

Heat a 10-to 12-inch cast-iron skillet or a griddle pan on the flat side until nearly smoking hot. Turn on your kitchen vent.

Cook the tofu in small batches, careful not to crowd the pan, for 3 to 5 minutes per side. The tofu will darken in color and maybe even look slightly blackened; this is a good thing. You'll probably switch back and forth between medium and medium-high heat throughout the cooking. Wipe the skillet with a dry towel of any lingering burnt bits.

Transfer the tofu to a baking sheet and keep in the oven until you're ready to serve, along with the red beans and brown rice.

MAKES 8 SERVINGS. YOU MAY HALVE THE AMOUNTS FOR A SMALLER PARTY.

- 2 (14-ounce) packages fresh extra-firm tofu, preferably organic
- ¾ teaspoon cayenne
- ¾ teaspoon freshly ground black pepper
- 1 tablespoon smoked paprika
- 1 tablespoon garlic powder
- 1 tablespoon onion powder
- 1 tablespoon dried thyme
- 1 tablespoon dried oregano
- 2½ teaspoons salt
- Neutral oil, for brushing

TOOLS: *10- or 12-inch cast-iron skillet or smooth-surfaced griddle*

CREOLE-STYLE BREAD PUDDING WITH BOOZY CITRUS SAUCE **V**

- Oil or butter, to grease your baking dish
- 1 (12-ounce) package soft or firm silken tofu, preferably organic or non-GMO
- 1 tablespoon vanilla extract
- 1 very ripe banana
- ½ cup plus 1 tablespoon brown or granulated sugar
- 1 (13-ounce can) coconut milk
- 1 teaspoon ground cinnamon
- ¼ teaspoon grated nutmeg
- Pinch of salt
- Zest of 1 orange
- 1 large stale (but not rock-hard) baguette or country-style loaf, cut into 1-inch pieces (for a total of 6 cups)
- Topping: 1 to 2 ripe bananas, sliced, or ¼ cup shaved bittersweet chocolate

Tool: Food processor or blender, baking dish at least 13- by 9-inches

Look for the silken tofu packaged in shelf-stable boxes, often found on the shelves with Asian ingredients in conventional supermarkets. Choose either the soft or firm variety. If you've got a black banana sitting in your freezer, now's a perfect time to use it. Day-old bread is ideal for this preparation, so that it can more effectively sop up the "pudding." To "stale" fresh bread, cut as directed, place on a baking sheet in a single layer and place in the oven at 300°F for up to an hour, making sure they're not turning into croutons.

HERE'S WHAT YOU DO:

Grease a baking dish that's at least 13- by 9-inches (a smaller dish will result in deep layers of pudding that take forever to bake).

Place the tofu, vanilla, banana, sugar, and coconut milk in a food processor or blender and puree. Add the cinnamon, nutmeg, salt, and orange zest, and process until well blended.

Place the bread in a large bowl and pour the sweet puree on top, stirring with a rubber spatula until the bread is completely coated. Let sit for at least 30 minutes.

Preheat the oven to 350°F.

Transfer the bread pudding to the prepared dish. Top with the sliced bananas or shaved chocolate (they're equally good; the chocolate does give nice color on top and the results are not chocolaty).

Place the dish on a baking sheet and into the oven. Bake for 55 to 60 minutes; the pudding should be somewhat firm and golden on top.

Allow to cool for at least 10 minutes before serving.

Serve warm or at room temperature, with or without the boozy citrus sauce. Keep leftovers in the refrigerator; reheat gently.

MAKES 10 TO 12 SERVINGS

SLIGHTLY BOOZY CITRUS SAUCE

HERE'S WHAT YOU DO:

In a small saucepan (think deep rather than shallow) over medium-low heat, stir the sugar until melted. Stop stirring, allowing the sugar to turn a deep mahogany color. This may happen very quickly. In the absence of stirring, you may swirl the pan to move the sugar and take it off the heat.

Add the vinegar and stir vigorously. At first, the mixture will harden, but don't fret; keep stirring—the caramel will melt within a few minutes.

Add the juice and liquor of choice and bring the mixture to a boil, stirring regularly. The mixture will reduce and thicken over the next 8 to 10 minutes.

To serve, spoon 1 tablespoon of sauce onto a plate, then place the bread pudding on top.

MAKES ENOUGH FOR 8 TO 10 SERVINGS

- 6 tablespoons granulated sugar
- 1 tablespoon balsamic or sherry vinegar
- ¼ cup orange or blood orange juice
- ¼ cup rum or bourbon

LUNAR NEW YEAR

A multiday celebration that begins on the first day of the lunar calendar, Lunar New Year is celebrated in China, Hong Kong, and Taiwan, as well as Vietnam (where the holiday is referred to as Tet) and Korea, which also observes the solar/Gregorian New Year's on January 1. It's an auspicious time, and food plays a central role in the festivities and preparation for the year to come. Even in the absence of regional traditions, long noodles represent longevity in Chinese tradition, and as such are an important element of a New Year's feast. To that end, I serve up my take on long noodles with the singularly flavored salted black soybeans, along with some bok choy (the greens are said to open the door to good fortune and prosperity). The menu is a pan-Asian sampler platter, with additional nods to Vietnam and Thailand, where Songkran, the Thai lunar celebration, is celebrated in mid-April. On their own, these dishes can easily translate into weeknight fare, but as an ensemble make a splendid buffet at any time of the year.

THAI CURRIED COLLARDS V GF

From Savannah to Shanghai, greens are important in both Western and Lunar New Year's feasts—a bit of culinary wishful thinking for prosperity and good fortune. Although collard greens typically don't show up in Asian dishes, they do a masterful job in this curry. If a New Year's feast is not in your plans, I still urge you to try this on a weeknight when some belly warming is in order. Besides, it's another excuse for playing with one of Mother Nature's most nutritionally endowed vegetables.

HERE'S WHAT YOU DO:

In small batches, stack the collards in a pile, roll up like a cigar, and cut into thin ribbonlike strips. (This technique is called to chiffonade.)

Over medium heat, heat the oil in a medium-size pot fitted with a lid. (A wok works great.) Add the shallots and ginger and allow them to dance in the oil and soften slightly, stirring frequently to prevent burning or sticking, about 3 minutes. Add the curry paste, stirring to blend everything together, about 1 minute.

In batches, add the collards, turning with tongs to coat with the aromatics. Collards need more time to shrink and wilt than do quick-cooking greens such as spinach and chard; it may take up to 10 minutes to turn and coat all of the greens. Season the greens with ½ teaspoon of the salt and a slight squeeze of the lime half.

Pour in the coconut milk plus ½ cup of the water; the level of liquid will be slightly lower than the vegetables. Increase the heat to medium-high, and bring the mixture up to a boil. Lower the heat to medium-low, cover, and simmer until the greens are as tender as you like them, 25 to 30 minutes. If you'd like a thinner sauce, add the remaining ½ cup of water while the greens simmer.

Taste for salt, and add more as needed, plus an additional squeeze of lime.

Serve in a bowl (with or without brown rice) so you can lap up some of the lip-smacking sauce.

MAKES 6 SERVINGS

- 7 to 8 cups collard greens, washed thoroughly, trimmed of stems and middle ribs (about 2 bunches)
- 2 tablespoons oil
- ½ cup minced shallots (1 to 2 bulbs, depending on size)
- 1 tablespoon peeled and minced fresh ginger (about a 2 by 1-inch hunk)
- 2 to 3 tablespoons prepared Thai red curry paste, depending on how spicy you like things
- ½ to 1 teaspoon salt
- ½ lime
- 1 (13-ounce) can coconut milk
- ½ to 1 cup water

- 1 (14-ounce) package fresh extra-firm tofu, preferably organic
- 3 garlic cloves
- 1 tablespoon peeled and sliced fresh ginger
- 2 tablespoons minced lemongrass "hearts" (2 thick or 3 thin stalks)
- 2 tablespoons soy sauce or wheat-free tamari
- 1 teaspoon sesame oil
- 2 tablespoons neutral oil, plus more for brushing
- ½ pound carrots, peeled and cut into 3-inch matchsticks (about 2 cups)
- ½ teaspoon coriander seeds (optional but nice)
- ¾ cup distilled white vinegar
- 8 to 9 tablespoons water
- ½ teaspoon salt
- ½ teaspoon granulated sugar
- ½ cup all-natural creamy peanut butter
- 1 teaspoon sriracha chili sauce or your favorite hot sauce
- 3 tablespoons freshly squeezed lime juice (about 1 lime)
- 5 (4- to 5-inch-long) soft sandwich rolls, or 1 (2-foot-long) soft-crusted French-style loaf
- 1 medium-size cucumber, peeled and sliced into rounds
- ¼ to ½ cup cilantro leaves, washed and dried
- Optional for heat lovers: 1 medium-size jalapeño, sliced into rounds

KOD'S PB & BÁNH MÌ Ⓥ

If I was back home and asked to describe to another native Philadelphian what a *bánh mì* is, I'd have two words: Vietnamese hoagie. All of the elements are the same: a mix of meats, a special sauce, and savory fixin's all tucked into a long, soft roll. The Viet-style hoagie here is stuffed with lemongrass-scented pan-fried tofu, with a quick carrot pickle and a spicy "mayo" made with peanut butter. "Mì oh my!" is how tester Jim Eber described his two-foot-long work of art. I couldn't have said it better.

HERE'S WHAT YOU DO:

Drain the tofu: Remove from the package and place on a plate. Place a second plate on top and weigh the tofu down with something heavy, such as a can of tomatoes. Allow to sit for about 20 minutes.

Meanwhile, prepare the tofu marinade: Thinly slice one of the garlic cloves and pulverize with a mortar and pestle.* When pasty, add the ginger, followed by the lemongrass, and pound into a unified paste.

Place the spice paste in a small bowl, along with the soy sauce, sesame oil, and the 2 tablespoons of the neutral oil, and with a fork, whisk everything together.

Lay the tofu on a cutting surface, on one of its long sides. Cut in half on the diagonal so you have two large triangles. Lay each triangle half on its longest side, and from the top short edge, cut into four thinner triangles, ¼- to ½-inch thick, giving you a total of eight pieces. Then cut each smaller triangle in half, so that you have a grand total of sixteen pieces.

Place the tofu in a single layer in a shallow dish. With a brush, apply the marinade on both sides. Marinate in the refrigerator for 1 hour (it's okay to marinate for longer, up to several hours).

Meanwhile, make the carrot pickle: Thinly slice the remaining two cloves of garlic and place them in a medium-size bowl, along with the carrot matchsticks.

In a small saucepan, combine the vinegar, 4 tablespoons of the water, the salt, and the sugar, and bring to a boil, making sure that the salt and sugar are dissolved. Pour the brine over the carrot mixture and allow to steep for a minimum of 45 minutes.

While the carrots "pickle," make the peanut butter "mayo": Place the peanut butter in a small bowl and stir vigorously until somewhat whipped in appearance. Stir in the sriracha, followed by the lime juice, then 4 tablespoons of the water. The mixture will thicken and seize and maybe even look as if it's curdling before it loosens up again and returns to its naturally creamy state. The mouthfeel will be quite voluptuous. Stir in the remaining 1 tablespoon of water if the sauce is thicker than you'd like.

Prep the tofu for panfrying: Brush with oil on both sides. Over medium-high heat, get a large (think wide and shallow) skillet very hot. (The pan is hot enough when a bead of water vaporizes instantly.) Add the tofu in small batches and cook until golden brown, 2 to 3 minutes on each side. Transfer to a paper towel to drain. Wipe the skillet of any burnt lemongrass bits before adding more tofu.

Assembly: Slice the bread in half lengthwise. Gently remove some of the bread innards to create a nest for the sandwich fillings. Generously spread the peanut butter "mayo" on both sides of the bread; you will have extra for the table. Line the cucumber slices on one side, followed by the tofu, fitting snugly along the length of the bread. Remove some of the carrots from the brine and place on top of the tofu, followed by the cilantro. Heat lovers: Slice 1 medium-size jalapeno into rounds and place on top. Put some of the remaining carrots on the table; they will improve with flavor over time and will keep in the brine in a covered refrigerated container for at least 1 week.

Place the other bread half on top and press down to "glue." Cut into slices, and remember to share.

MAKES 5 ENTRÉE-SIZE OR 8 TO 10 SNACK-SIZE SERVINGS

TOOLS: *Mortar and pestle*

No mortar and pestle? Slice the garlic and lay the flat side of a chef's knife on top. With one hand on the handle (which is close to you, off the edge of cutting surface) and the palm of your other hand on top of the knife, press on the garlic in a smearing fashion. Repeat with the ginger and the lemongrass. You can also use a mini chopper.

KITCHEN NOTES: *Some wrangling is required for lemongrass. Remove the tough woody exterior, then slice off the upper blade portion, which is raspy. Use only the lower half of the stalk. Packaged stalks available in supermarket produce sections are a convenient, no-fuss option but can be less fragrant and flavorful than the stalk in its unprepped state. If lemongrass doesn't grow where you live, look for the entire stalks in Asian markets . . . or grow it yourself.*

Choose a soft French-style loaf with a light crumb, rather than a traditional baguette with a classically crisp crust.

LONG NOODLES WITH SALTED BLACK BEANS AND BOK CHOY ▯

- 12 ounces dried Chinese egg noodles or Italian spaghetti
- 3 tablespoons salted black beans, chopped finely
- ⅓ cup water
- 3 tablespoons Shaoxing rice wine or dry sherry
- 3 tablespoons soy sauce
- ¾ teaspoon granulated sugar
- 1½ teaspoons sesame oil
- 3 tablespoons neutral oil
- ⅓ cup minced shallot (2 to 3 bulbs)
- 1 tablespoon peeled and minced fresh ginger (a 2 by 1-inch hunk)
- 1 to 2 cloves garlic, minced
- ½ to ¾ fresh chile pepper of choice, seeded and minced, to taste
- 4 to 5 cups bok choy that has been washed and dried thoroughly, then cut into ½-inch pieces
- ¼ cup minced scallions, root and dark tops removed
- ¼ cup fresh cilantro leaves, chopped finely
- Sesame seeds, for garnish

TOOLS: *Wok or 12-inch-wide skillet*

KITCHEN NOTES: *Details on where to source and how to store salted black beans (also sold as fermented black beans) are in the Pantry section on page 8. Don't worry if you can't find the Chinese egg noodles; Italian spaghetti works as a great stand-in.*

Here's more from the culinary wish list: Eat a bowl of long noodles and you'll live a long life. I oblige with a decidedly homey albeit slurp-a-licious version, kicked up with pungent sauce of salted black beans, ginger, garlic, and soy sauce. And because we all can use a few extra bills, I add plenty of bok choy, a symbol of money. Like the Curried Collards (page 107), this is another weeknight winner.

HERE'S WHAT YOU DO:

Bring about 3 quarts of water to a boil and add the noodles. Cook for 6 to 7 minutes (or if cooking spaghetti, according to the package instructions). Drain and rinse under cold running water. (Spaghetti does not need to be rinsed.)

While the noodles cook, combine the black beans, water, rice wine, soy sauce, sugar, and sesame oil in a small bowl, and stir together. This is your sauce.

Heat a wok or 12-inch-wide skillet over medium-high heat until the pan is very hot, then swirl in the oil, coating the surface. Add the shallots and stir-fry, tossing and stirring, about 1 minute. Then add the ginger, garlic, and chile pepper, stir-frying for an additional 30 seconds. Add the bok choy, tossing to coat with the aromatics. Stir-fry for about 3 minutes; the greens will wilt and shrink. Add the sauce and bring to a boil, about 90 seconds.

Add the noodles, using both tongs and maybe even a large spoon to toss and coat the noodles with the sauce and the vegetable mixture. Keep the noodles moving until they are heated through.

Sprinkle the scallions on top, followed by the cilantro and the sesame seeds.

Serve while hot.

MAKES 6 SERVINGS

STOVETOP BROWN RICE GF

- 1 cup uncooked short-, medium-, or long-grain brown rice
- 1¾ cups water

There are infinite ways to cook a pot of brown rice. Some like to rinse the grains before cooking; others soak those rinsed grains as well. There are folks in the rice cooker camp and those, like yours truly, who swear by the boiled water/stovetop method. My friend Fuzzy has a trick that involves toasting the grains in one pot, boiling water in another, and mixing the two. The lesson learned: Do what works for you. Here's how it's done in our kitchen.

HERE'S WHAT YOU DO:

Bring the rice and the water to a boil in a medium-size saucepan. Cover and cook over low heat until the water is absorbed and the rice is tender to the bite. The cooking time for medium- and long-grain rice is 40 to 42 minutes. For short-grain rice, it's 38 to 40 minutes.

Keep covered off the heat for 5 minutes, or until ready to serve.

GENERALLY SPEAKING, 1 CUP UNCOOKED RICE YIELDS ABOUT 3 CUPS COOKED RICE.

TROPICAL FRUIT PLATE WITH CHILE-LIME SALT V GF KIDDO

I use a version of this seasoned salt with the strawberry and pepita salad (page 173), but in swapping out fine sea salt for coarser crystals, I end up with a completely different result that delivers major flavor kapow. If you've never had the pleasure of experiencing sel gris at home, this dish is an easy gateway to see what the fuss is all about.

HERE'S WHAT YOU DO:

Peel and cut up the pineapple: Cut off the bottom to create a flat edge, making the cutting easier and safe, then slice off the top.

From top to bottom, slice away the tough exterior, including the brown prickly bits.

Using the core as the focal point, visualize the pineapple as a four-sided object. Place the blade of your knife on the fleshy edge of the core and slice from top to bottom. You should have four large slabs of pineapple, with only the core remaining. Trim away any remaining brown prickly bits and skin.

Cut each pineapple slab into four or five spears, about ½-inch thick.

And, if using, peel and cut the mangoes: Hold a mango in an upright position, stem side up. Two larger, flatter sides and two smaller, curved sides surround the pit. Place the knife at the top of one of the flatter sides and slice from top to bottom. Repeat on the other flatter side. You will have two mango "cheeks." Cut each "cheek" into smaller slices, about 1-inch thick.

Slice off each of the smaller sides and slice into small pieces if needed.

Using a salt grinder or mortar and pestle, lightly grind the salt. Transfer to a small bowl, and stir in the lime zest, followed by the cayenne. Taste and add more if needed.

Divide the salt between two small, shallow spice bowls.

Arrange the fruit on a platter and pass the salt around the table. Dip the fruit directly into the salt or sprinkle on top.

MAKES 6 SERVINGS

- 1 to 2 ripe pineapples, and/or 2 ripe mangoes
- 2 tablespoons sel gris or another unrefined coarse salt
- Zest of 2 limes, minced
- ¼ teaspoon cayenne, or to taste

ISN'T IT ROMANTIC: TABLE FOR TWO, EVEN WHEN IT'S NOT VALENTINE'S DAY

As mentioned in the introduction to *The Meat Lover's Meatless Cookbook*, I got the attention of the man who would become my husband with a piece of fried chicken. Admittedly, it was an odd and bold move to make with a colleague. But I couldn't stop thinking about this nerdy guy from Kentucky and wanted him to read my thoughts as he opened the foil-wrapped package.

The timing was all wrong; I was about to move to the other side of the world to get married and he was newly separated from his first wife. But we were like peas and carrots, an unlikely combination that worked in spite of all the best-laid plans. One of the first things I noticed is that like me, he's a good sharer. Without hesitation, he'll give me a bite of his sandwich, an orange segment, a spoonful of ice cream; and that unconditional generosity is one of the things that made me fall in love with him. So what if he really couldn't cook; he could learn, as long as he was with me. But share? That's a rare quality that comes from within.

I am reminded of the oft-quoted line from *An Alphabet for Gourmets* by the late, great M. F. K. Fisher, who reminds us that "sharing food with another human being is an intimate act that should not be indulged in lightly."

Much has been said about culinary aphrodisiacs, from asparagus to oysters, chocolate to strawberries, and what they can do for our libido. I say, don't sweat the clinical details and just cook. It's one of the sexiest things you can do for your sweetheart, and the simpler the dish the better. As the late Bunny Crumpacker wrote in *The Sex Life of Food*, "Beauty is in the eye of the lover, thank goodness, and so we are all beautiful when we are well loved and even more so when we are also well fed."

These days, my copilot and I get equally excited over roasted tofu as we do over the occasional fried chicken that initially brought us together. With his help, I've combed the collection for the dishes that inspire sharing between two lovers on that first, tenth, or ten-thousandth dinner date.

Kitchen notes: Most of the recipes in the book make six servings. For a table for two, you may reduce the ingredient amounts by half.

SAINT PATRICK'S DAY

With a name like O'Donnel, my including a menu for this holiday was a given. But the challenge was identifying savory alternatives to a quintessential "roast beast"—corned beef and cabbage—beloved by my meat-loving brethren with similarly sounding surnames. My friend Fuzzy likes to say that kale is the "steak" of the plant world, and when it's massaged with garlic, lemon, olive oil, and almonds, it's got a lip-smacking quality that truly bolsters his argument. Its partner is a pie of mashed potatoes that slices ever so nicely and easily eaten out of hand at room temperature, along with a green beer. You won't need to wear that KISS ME, I'M IRISH T-shirt; guests will love you after tucking into the Guinness-powered gingerbread that could end up becoming a new tradition. Who said Saint Pat couldn't go meatless?

SPLIT PEAS AND CARROTS (AND TURNIPS, TOO) STEW V GF

What stands out about this dish (along with the potato pie that follows) is its willful determination to be perfectly pleasant. Neither assertive nor shy in flavor, neither too chunky nor too brothy in consistency, this stew is a perfect example of a dish that practices moderation. In a world where cooks are in constant pursuit of the biggest, brightest flavors, here's a mild-mannered break against convention, in which the ingredients—many of them earthy—speak for themselves. Besides, it's another chance to share my love for the maligned turnip (it's featured in the blue cheesy gratin on page 63). Paired with the pie, this little number takes the chill off a late winter's eve.

HERE'S WHAT YOU DO:

In a medium-size saucepan or soup pot fitted with a lid, heat the oil over medium heat and add the onion and garlic. Stir to keep from sticking and burning and cook until softened, about 5 minutes. Stir in the ginger, then add the peas, stirring until coated with the aromatics. Then add the coriander, paprika, and the ½ teaspoon of salt, stirring to coat the peas. The mixture may be slightly pasty; that's okay.

Pour in 7 cups of the water. Increase the heat to medium-high and bring the mixture to a boil. Lower the heat to medium-low, cover, and cook for about 15 minutes.

Meanwhile, bring the remaining 4 cups of water to a boil in a small saucepan. Add the carrots and turnips and cook for 4 minutes. Remove with a slotted spoon or drain over a sieve. Transfer the vegetables to the pot of peas, and stir.

Cook the stew until the peas are tender to the bite, an additional 20 to 25 minutes. Stir in the mustard, plus additional salt and black pepper to taste. You may need to stir for a few minutes until the mustard dissolves.

Sprinkle each bowl with the lemon zest and parsley, and serve hot.

MAKES 6 TO 8 SERVINGS

- 2 tablespoons olive oil
- ½ medium-size onion, chopped (about ¾ cup)
- 2 to 3 garlic cloves, minced
- 1 (1 by 1-inch) piece fresh ginger, peeled and minced (about 1 tablespoon)
- 2 cups dried split green peas
- 1 teaspoon ground coriander
- ½ teaspoon paprika or other medium-heat ground chile pepper
- ½ teaspoon salt, plus more to taste
- 11 cups water
- 2 cups combined carrot and turnip, peeled and cut into ½-inch-cubes
- 1 tablespoon Dijon mustard
- Freshly ground black pepper
- Zest of 1 lemon, minced, for garnish
- ½ cup fresh parsley, chopped, for garnish

RAW KALE SALAD `DO`

"You know, Kim, right? Kim-with-the-kale-salad-Kim?" That's how I was recently introduced to the neighbor of a friend, who had shared this salad during rounds of recipe testing. For fear of waxing too poetic, this salad has the power to change your life, to turn you on your cruciferous-hating head, and spread the love for kale in all its natural glory. Honestly, I can't take the credit; Mother Nature really does the talking here.

HERE'S WHAT YOU DO:

Wash the kale leaves and dry thoroughly in a salad spinner. Stack several leaves in a small pile and cut into thin strips (also known as to chiffonade).

Place the chopped kale in a medium-size bowl and add the lemon juice, olive oil, garlic, and salt. With your hands, massage the seasonings into the kale; this not only ensures even coverage but also helps tenderize the raw greens. Allow the greens to sit and marinate for at least 20 minutes.

Toss in the almonds, and taste. There is usually so much flavor that the cheese and bread crumbs are unnecessary, but they are terrific extras that really gild the lily.

Keeps for 2 days in the refrigerator.

MAKES ABOUT 6 SIDE-DISH SERVINGS

- 1 bunch lacinato kale (also sold as Tuscan and dinosaur kale), middle ribs removed (about 5 cups)
- 3 tablespoons freshly squeezed lemon juice (from 1 to 2 lemons, depending on size)
- ¼ cup olive oil
- 1 clove garlic, minced
- ½ teaspoon salt
- ¼ cup unsalted almonds, chopped

OPTIONAL ADD-ONS:
- ¼ cup grated Parmigiano-Reggiano or pecorino cheese
- ¼ to ⅓ cup dried bread crumbs

TOOLS: *Salad spinner*

- 2 pounds russet potatoes or medium-starch varieties (e.g., Yellow Finn or Yukon Gold), scrubbed well, trimmed, peeled as needed, and quartered (about 5 medium-size potatoes)
- 2 teaspoons salt
- 2 cloves garlic, peeled and left whole
- 4 cups water
- 3 tablespoons olive oil
- Medium-grain cornmeal, for dusting pan
- 1 egg
- ½ cup grated Parmigiano-Reggiano
- 1 teaspoon dried oregano
- Freshly ground black pepper
- ½ cup unseasoned dried bread crumbs of your choice (the flaky texture of panko is nice)

TOOLS: *Handheld potato masher, 9-inch round pie pan*

POTATO PIE   KIDDO

Like its split pea compatriot, this pie of embellished mashed potatoes is an exemplar of no-nonsense comfort food. I love how it truly eats like a pie that you can slice and eat with a fork or out of hand. When the weather warms up, this makes terrific picnic fare.

HERE'S WHAT YOU DO:

In a medium-size saucepan fitted with a lid, combine the potatoes, salt, and garlic. Pour in the water, cover, and bring to a boil. Lower the heat to low and cook the potatoes for 25 minutes, or until fork tender.

While the potatoes cook, preheat the oven to 350°F. Brush 1 tablespoon of the olive oil on the bottom and sides of a 9-inch pie pan. Lightly dust the bottom of the pan with about ⅛ cup of the cornmeal.

In a small bowl, beat the egg with a fork, then add the cheese.

Transfer the potatoes and garlic to a large mixing bowl, reserving the cooking liquid. With a handheld masher, mash the potatoes and add the remaining 2 tablespoons of olive oil, which both lubricates and seasons the hot potatoes. If the potatoes seem dry, gradually ladle in some of the reserved cooking water, but please exercise caution, as you want to avoid a soupy mess.

With a wooden spoon or rubber spatula, stir in the cheese mixture, then add the oregano, black pepper, and bread crumbs.

Transfer the mixture to the prepared pan, place on a baking sheet, and bake on the middle rack for 40 to 45 minutes, until the top is golden brown.

Allow to cool for at least 5 minutes, then with a pie server, cut into wedges. Eat hot or at room temperature.

MAKES 8 TO 10 SERVINGS

GUINNESS GINGERBREAD

Brit kitchen minx Nigella Lawson's Guinness-flavored chocolate cake (and cream cheese frosting) has become a family "please, pretty please" favorite. Using Lawson's brilliant stovetop batter method, I've come up with a spice-forward variation that has earned high marks from the cake lovers' club. The sweetened Greek yogurt "whipped cream" kicks Cool Whip to the curb.

- 2 cups all-purpose flour
- 2 teaspoons baking soda
- 2 teaspoons ground ginger
- 1 teaspoon ground cinnamon
- ¼ teaspoon ground cloves
- 1 egg
- ¼ cup unsulfured molasses
- ¼ cup honey
- 1¼ cups 2% or "traditional" full-fat plain Greek yogurt
- 4 tablespoons butter
- ½ cup light or dark brown sugar
- 1 cup Irish stout or porter-style ale
- 3 to 4 tablespoons confectioners' sugar

TOOLS: *Parchment paper, 8- or 9-inch round cake pan, balloon whisk*

KITCHEN NOTES: *No Greek yogurt in your neck of the woods? Place a metal sieve over a bowl and pour plain yogurt into the sieve, letting it drain for 30 minutes or so.*

HERE'S WHAT YOU DO:

Preheat the oven to 350°F. Grease an 8- or 9-inch round cake pan, then line it with parchment paper, with a few inches of overhang so you can easily remove the cake after it's cooled.

In a medium-size bowl, combine the flour, baking soda, ginger, cinnamon, and cloves, and stir until well mixed.

In another medium-size bowl, whisk together the egg, molasses, honey, and ¾ cup of the yogurt, until well blended.

Melt the butter in a medium-size or large saucepan over medium-low heat. Add the brown sugar and stir until the sugar is dissolved. Add the beer and bring to a boil. Whisk in the molasses mixture, lowering the heat to low. Switch to a wooden spoon, and carefully add the dry ingredients, stirring vigorously until the flour flecks are gone. You may finish stirring off the heat.

Pour the batter into the prepared pan, place on a baking sheet, and bake for 30 minutes, or until a skewer inserted in the middle of the cake emerges fairly cleanly (it's okay if there's a little residue).

Let cool in the pan for about 30 minutes, then lift the cake out of the pan using the parchment overhang. Transfer to a cooling rack, then peel off the parchment after an hour of cooling.

While the cake cools, make the "whipped cream": Place the remaining ½ cup of yogurt in a medium-size bowl, along with 3 tablespoons of the confectioners' sugar, and whisk vigorously. The yogurt will loosen and whip quite readily. Taste for sweetness, and add more sugar as needed.

Serve at room temperature, with a dollop of "whipped cream."

MAKES AT LEAST 12 SLICES

SPRING

when the birds come back
from vacation

SPRING FORWARD FEAST

Behold the sun! It's coming home, thanks to the equinox and government-issue daylight saving time. That alone is cause for celebration. The plants are rejoicing, too; with longer days come tender greens, soft-bulbed onions, and before you know it, spears of asparagus, the ultimate edible harbinger of baseball season. (and Frisbee! And bike rides!) The menu is awash in green, but hearty enough to keep off the evening chill that lingers for a while longer. The soup can work on its own as midweek sustenance, and is a great companion for either the barley-spinach pilaf (a.k.a. Spanako-barley) or the kale pesto–lathered pasta and white beans. Jam-dot cookies get a gluten-free makeover that is undetectable. Who's up for an Earth Day lunch?

JUMBO PASTA SHELLS WITH KALE PESTO AND WHITE BEANS   KIDDO

Here's another one that screams, "Spring is here!" albeit ever so cautiously. The white beans and lemon zest are strutting their optimistic selves, but the kale pesto is a reminder that cool-weather crops are still de rigueur and that hearty suppers are necessary to take the chill off. It's been fun to come up with a new way to use jumbo pasta shells, which typically are stuffed and drowning in marinara sauce.

HERE'S WHAT YOU DO:

Kale Pesto

Bring the water to a boil. Add 1 teaspoon of the salt, then add the kale. Cook uncovered until tender, about 10 minutes. Drain the kale under cold running water. With your hands, squeeze as much water out of the kale as possible; you'll end up with a green ball about the size of a tennis ball.

In a blender or food processor, combine the walnuts and garlic, and whiz until pulverized and well mixed. Add the kale and process until well blended; the mixture may even look a little dry. Pour in the oil and blend. The mixture should be glistening and will have a consistency that is somewhat textured, somewhat loose. Taste and add the remaining ½ teaspoon of salt, if needed.

Transfer the pesto to a small bowl and stir in the cheese (if using) and the black pepper.

Pesto keeps well in an airtight container in the refrigerator, for up to a week.

MAKES ABOUT 1 CUP PESTO

Beans 'n' Shells

Place the beans in a bowl and cover with about 3 inches of water. Soak for at least 4 hours. (In warmer climes, soak the beans in the refrigerator to avoid sprouting or fermentation.)

▶ ▶ ▶

KALE PESTO:

- 4 cups water
- 1 to 1½ teaspoons salt
- 4 cups lacinato (a.k.a. dinosaur or Tuscan) kale that has been stemmed and chopped coarsely
- ¼ cup unsalted walnuts, chopped
- 2 cloves garlic, minced
- ½ cup olive oil
- ½ cup grated Parmigiano-Reggiano cheese (optional)
- Freshly ground black pepper

TOOLS: *Food processor or stand blender*

BEANS 'N' SHELLS:

- 1¼ cups dried white beans
- 2 cloves garlic, peeled and left whole
- 3 teaspoons salt, plus more to taste
- 1 (12-ounce) box jumbo pasta shells
- ¾ to 1 cup kale pesto
- ½ cup Parmigiano-Reggiano cheese, grated
- Zest of 2 lemons
- Freshly ground black pepper

TOOLS: *Slotted spoon*

Drain the beans. Transfer to a medium-size or large pot fitted with a lid and cover with at least 6 cups of water; you're looking for a few inches of water above the beans. Add the garlic and bring to a boil. Cook at a hard boil for 5 minutes. Cover, lower the heat, and cook at a gentle simmer. At minute 20, stir in 1 teaspoon of the salt.

At minute 45, check the beans for doneness. Cook in 10-minute increments until the beans are tender to the bite, keeping in mind that cooking times may vary, depending on the age of the beans.

Transfer the beans to a bowl, along with about half of the cooking liquid.

In a medium-size or large pot fitted with a lid, bring 6 cups of water to a boil and add the remaining 2 teaspoons of salt. Cook the shells for 14 minutes at a moderate boil. Turn off the heat, cover, and let the shells cook passively for 7 minutes. Remove with a slotted spoon or a pair of tongs, checking for lingering water, and transfer to a medium-size bowl.

Add ½ cup of the kale pesto and gently stir to completely coat the shells. Dust the shells with ¼ cup of the cheese (if using) followed by half of the lemon zest and black pepper to your liking.

When ready to serve, gently reheat the beans over low heat in a saucepan or in a microwave.

To serve, place five to six shells on each plate or in shallow bowls. Top each serving of shells with ½ cup of the beans, drained, followed by 1 teaspoon of pesto and a sprinkling of both lemon zest and cheese.

Eat hot.

MAKES 6 SERVINGS

KITCHEN NOTES: *I am yet again pushing dried beans and the extra steps that come with them. The texture is so much meatier than their canned counterparts and I reckon they sop up that pesto a whole lot better, too.*

You can make both the pesto (warning: addictive stuff) and beans in advance, and make the shells just before you're ready to sit down. The dusting of Parmigiano-Reggiano is completely optional, but cheese lovers will agree that a little goes a long way here.

My hope for the pasta shells was to break against tradition and refrain from stuffing, saucing, and baking them. But I had to work around the cooking instructions on the pasta package, which are specifically designed for baked stuffed shells. When the shells are boiled, then passively cooked off the heat in their cooking water, they turn out tender without tearing, a perfect centerpiece for the pesto and white beans.

On prepping the kale: Grab the thick fibrous stem running through the middle and simply pull off the leafy part. You can also run a knife along the middle and trim the leaf away from the stem.

SPRING FORWARD SOUP DO

- ½ pound medium-starch potatoes (Yellow Finn or Yukon Gold) or russet potatoes, peeled and quartered (1 to 2 medium-size potatoes)
- 2 cloves garlic, peeled and left whole
- ½ to 1½ teaspoons salt, to taste
- 7 cups water
- 3 tablespoons olive oil
- ½ pound leeks, white and light green parts only, washed thoroughly and cut into ½-inch rounds (about 2 medium-size leeks)
- ½ pound fennel bulb, fronds and root removed, cut into ½-inch-thick slices
- ½ pound asparagus, woody ends removed, cut into 2- or 3-inch pieces (about 1 bunch)
- 3 to 5 sprigs fresh thyme
- 1 Parmigiano-Reggiano or pecorino cheese rind (optional but nice)
- 7 cups spinach, washed thoroughly and stemmed
- Freshly ground black pepper
- Zest of 1 lemon, minced, plus juice of ½ lemon

You know that loving feeling when spring arrives and teases us for a hot second with a choir of songbirds and a whiff of daffodils? Then just like that, Mother Nature changes her mind and bursts our happy bubble with howling winds and raw rain. (There's a reason Ella Fitzgerald sang "Spring Can Really Hang You Up the Most"!) If you want to kick the spring blahs in the pants, make this soup. Chock-full of spring produce debutantes, it is green through and through, delivering the promise of bright, sunshiny tomorrows.

HERE'S WHAT YOU DO:

Place the potatoes, garlic, ½ teaspoon of the salt, and 2 cups of the water in a medium-size pot fitted with a lid and bring to a boil. Cover, lower the heat to medium-low, and cook until the potatoes are fork tender, about 19 minutes.

While the potatoes are cooking, warm the oil in a large, heavy-bottomed pot over medium-high heat. Add the leeks and fennel and stir to coat with the oil. Cook until softened, about 7 minutes. It's okay if the leeks get slightly golden in the process. Add the asparagus and toss with tongs until coated with the oil and the other vegetables. Add the thyme, cheese rind (if using), and the remaining 5 cups of water (should be at the same level as the vegetables) and bring the mixture to a boil.

Lower the heat to low and cook at a simmer for about 10 minutes; the asparagus should be just about fork tender. Place the spinach on top and allow to wilt, 3 to 5 minutes. Remove the thyme sprigs and the remains of the cheese rind, then add the potatoes and the garlic, reserving the cooking liquid.

Using an immersion or stand blender, puree the mixture until there are no lumps. Return the puree to the stove over low heat and taste for salt, adding the remaining 1 teaspoon in increments as needed. If the mixture is too thick, gradually ladle in some of the potato cooking liquid. Add black pepper to taste. Gradually add the lemon juice, tasting after every addition.

Garnish each serving with a sprinkling of lemon zest. Serve hot.

Crostini garnish option: Preheat the oven to 350°F. Cut the baguette half into a dozen superthin slices (two per serving)—about ⅛-inch thick, if possible. Place the bread on a baking sheet and into the oven, and allow to crisp, about 8 minutes.

Spread a thin layer of the goat cheese on each hot toast, with the remaining lemon zest, and place one in the middle of each bowl, the rest for the table.

MAKES 6 TO 8 STARTER-SIZE SERVINGS

TOOLS: *Immersion or stand blender*

KITCHEN NOTES: *In the spirit of efficiency, this is a two-pot affair, not a secret plot to dirty another pot. The potatoes, which act as the "cream" in this soup, happily cook by themselves in salted starchy water and are added to the mix of quick-cooking green vegetables, just before everything gets pureed.*

Feel free to use a mix of quick-wilting greens in addition to the spinach, including Swiss chard, tatsoi, or watercress for a peppery bite. Silt likes to linger inside the leeks, so make sure you look under the exterior layer, where it tends to congregate.

The addition of the cheese rind is completely optional but will add a flavor dimension and enhanced mouthfeel that will make meat lovers happy.

GOAT CHEESE CROSTINI OPTION:

- ½ baguette
- 4 to 6 ounces plain spreadable goat cheese

- 5 tablespoons olive oil
- 2 cups finely chopped red or yellow onion (not quite 1 large onion)
- 2 garlic cloves, peeled and chopped
- 1 cup pearl barley
- 1 pound fresh spinach (about 8 cups), washed, trimmed, and chopped coarsely (chard is a great substitute)
- ½ teaspoon salt
- 1½ cups water
- 1 cup chopped fresh dill
- ⅛ teaspoon grated nutmeg
- Juice of 1 lemon
- ¼ pound feta cheese
- Freshly ground black pepper

SPANAKO-BARLEY

In my quest to swap out white rice for whole grains, I consulted cookbook author Maria Speck, author of the much-lauded *Ancient Grains, Modern Meals*, for her thoughts on applying this idea to *spanakorizo*, the classic Greek spinach and (white) rice pilaf. I had my sights on barley, which Speck tells me, remains an important grain in Greece. I'm thrilled with the results, both toothy and creamy.

HERE'S WHAT YOU DO:

In a large soup pot fitted with a lid, heat the olive oil and cook the onions over medium-low heat for 7 to 8 minutes, until softened. Do not brown. Add the garlic, stir for 1 to 2 minutes, then add the barley and stir to coat with the oil and aromatics, 1 to 2 minutes.

Add the spinach in batches of about 2 cups, turning and coating with tongs after each addition, until wilted. Season with the salt. Add the water. Lower the heat to low, cover, and cook at a simmer for 30 minutes. Add the dill and nutmeg and gently stir in, also checking on the moisture level of the mixture. The end result should be smooth and creamy, so it's okay to add 1 or 2 tablespoons of water.

Cook for an additional 20 minutes. Turn off the heat, add the lemon juice and olive oil, and allow the barley to cook passively for 5 minutes.

Sprinkle or grate on the feta, depending on how hard or soft it is. Serve either warm or at room temperature.

MAKES 4 HEARTY ENTRÉE SERVINGS OR 6 SIDE-DISH PORTIONS

- 1 cup whole or slivered roasted, unsalted almonds
- 1 cup old-fashioned or quick-cooking oats (don't use instant)
- ½ cup whole beige quinoa, or ⅔ cup quinoa flour
- 1 teaspoon ground cinnamon
- ¼ cup neutral oil
- ½ cup good-quality pure maple syrup
- ½ cup freshly squeezed orange juice (from 2 to 3 oranges)
- 1 teaspoon vanilla extract
- ⅓ to ½ cup of your favorite homemade jam or marmalade, chilled

TOOLS: *Parchment paper, electric coffee or spice grinder, food processor*

JAM-DOT COOKIES V GF KIDDO

The inspiration for this recipe comes from the Golden Door Spa, in Escondido, California, where the jam-dot cookie is a signature treat beloved by guests. As these were already egg- and dairy-free, I set out to turn them into gluten-free morsels as well. With the encouragement of tester Susan Mack, who loves any chance to bake without wheat, I added ground quinoa to the equation. As with the brownies on page 97, the quinoa works great as a floury stand-in—not to mention the extra boost of protein and fiber!

HERE'S WHAT YOU DO:

Line a baking sheet with parchment paper.

Pulverize the almonds and oats in a food processor into a medium-coarse meal. Transfer to a large bowl.

Grind the quinoa in an electric coffee or spice grinder until it looks powdery, like flour. (No such grinder? Try a mini chopper or heavy-duty blender instead.) Add to the almond mixture, followed by the cinnamon, and stir together until well blended.

In a separate bowl, combine the oil, maple syrup, orange juice, and vanilla, and stir well.

With a rubber stirring spatula, incorporate the wet ingredients into the dry ingredients, and mix well. Cover the batter with plastic and refrigerate for 1 hour.

Preheat the oven to 375°F.

Scoop the batter with a 1-tablespoon measure and arrange, with space in between rows, on the prepared pan.

Using your thumb or the back of a spoon, make an indentation into the middle of each round. Fill the middle with a ¼ teaspoon of jam or marmalade.

Bake until golden brown around the edges, about 22 minutes. With a lifting spatula, transfer the cookies to a cooling rack.

The cookies are slightly soft and moist and keep best in a metal tin, for about 5 days.

MAKES 27 TO 30 COOKIES

KITCHEN NOTES: *Good-quality pure maple syrup means no high-fructose corn syrup in the mix. The good stuff does cost more but you'll be able to understand the difference when the first bit of maple-y nectar hits your lips.*

I recommend whole quinoa that you grind yourself at home, versus quinoa flour, which is costly, more difficult to find, and oxidizes quickly. For this recipe, use quinoa that's been rinsed before packaging. Ancient Harvest, Bob's Red Mill, Earthly Delights, and Eden Foods all sell rinsed quinoa, as stated on their labels.

The jam is entirely cook's choice, but it's a blast to use jam from your own pantry. I've included how-to details on pages 205–209 for a few different kinds.

A note about oats: For folks with celiac disease and gluten intolerance, make sure to use oats that are certified gluten-free.

EASTER

An Episcopal church in a small town southeast of Philadelphia is where my mother dutifully took me and my rambunctious kid brothers most Sundays. With religion as the backdrop, church was, for much of my youth, a hub of social activity that included pancake (and sausage) breakfasts, Christmas pageant rehearsals, and the Palm Sunday parade. We knew Lent as the time to give up something we loved and we knew it had something to do with the story of the death and resurrection of Jesus Christ. But we were also big believers in the Easter Bunny, which magically hopped his way into our house, gifting us each a pastel-colored basket of egg-shaped chocolates and jelly beans. Pictures were snapped, then off to church we would go. Easter dinner was always at the great-aunt and uncle's house, with ham (studded with cloves and glazed with 7UP) and French-fried string bean casserole on the menu. If we were lucky, it would be warm enough to run in the yard in our Easter finery.

For a beast-less Easter feast, my picks include:

EASTER EGG RADISH SNACK

I'm crazy for the shades of Easter . . . candy. Robin's egg blue,
strawberry pink, violet, daffodil yellow—they all make me swoon.
(I just wish I could keep my hands out of the candy bowl.) A few
years ago, I became acquainted with the Easter egg radish, and effectively found a new way to get my pastel fix. Available in dreamy
(or is that ice creamy?) shades of magenta, violet, lipstick red, and
creamy white, this variety of spring radish is a sight to behold after
the long winter. Mild yet peppery with plenty of crunch, the Easter
egg is a terrific prelude to a big meal, at just 20 calories per cup.

HERE'S WHAT YOU DO:

Cut the radishes into halves or quarters and place in a bowl or on a
tray. Place the salt and oil in separate dishes and arrange next to the
radishes. Dip the radishes in either the salt and/or the oil and enjoy.

Radish Crostini

Cut the radishes into ⅛-inch slices. Spread a small amount of butter on
each slice of bread, just enough to cover the surface. Place a few radish slices on top so they adhere to the butter. Sprinkle with the coarse
salt and serve.

MAKES AT LEAST 6 SERVINGS

- 2 bunches Easter Egg radishes,
  washed and trimmed of green tops
- Coarse salt, such as Maldon flakes
  or sel gris, for dipping
- Extra-virgin olive oil, for dipping

PLAN B: RADISH CROSTINI

- 1 baguette, cut into ¼-inch slices
- 4 tablespoons butter, softened

PASSOVER

Also known as Pesach, Passover is the Jewish holiday commemorating the freeing of Israelite slaves and the exodus from Egypt. It's a moving biblical story rich in culinary symbolism that plays out both at the seder table (first and sometimes second night of Passover) and throughout the eight-day observance. Perhaps the most widely practiced tradition is abstaining from *chametz*, which refers to anything made from wheat, rye, barley, oats, and spelt, and which has not cooked within 18 minutes upon contact with water. Although made from wheat, matzo is an unleavened cracker that fills these requirements and is eaten throughout Passover. I've taken said cracker and used it as a "noodle" in this lasagna (from *The Meat Lover's Meatless Cookbook*), which is a great option for dairy-loving vegetarians. That said, Passover is the one time of year to assume nothing and to check with your fellow diners on how strictly they observe this major holiday. In some households, for example, only "kosher for Passover" ingredients and specially designated dishware will suffice; in others, the rules are more relaxed. In recent years, quinoa has earned a place on the Passover table, as it's technically an unleavened grain, but, again, it's important to consult your tablemates if the Quinoa-Walnut Brownies are acceptable fare. All three types of the cheese used in this lasagna are available kosher for Passover; a few online kosher supermarkets are noted in the Resources section on page 216. As one Jewish tester noted, although unlikely she'd make this for a seder, she's looking forward to adding this to the Passover week rotation.

ARUGULA MATZO LASAGNA

HERE'S WHAT YOU DO:

Make the marinara sauce: In a medium-size saucepan, heat 2 table-spoons of the olive oil over medium heat, then add the onion, the minced garlic, and the carrot, cooking until slightly softened, about 5 minutes. Add the herbs and wine, if using; cook until the wine is reduced by half. Stir occasionally to minimize sticking.

Add the tomato puree and stir to combine. Bring to a boil, then lower the heat, so the sauce can simmer over low heat. Cover the pot and cook for about 30 minutes; remove the herb sprigs and add salt and pepper to taste. Keep warm until ready to assemble the lasagna.

Meanwhile, make the arugula filling: Divide the arugula in half and place in two bowls. At first, it will seem like an excessive amount of greens, but it will all be put to use.

Heat 1 tablespoon of the olive oil in a 12-inch skillet or wok over medium-high heat and add half of the arugula, and the 3 cloves of garlic sliced thinly. With tongs, turn the arugula to coat it with the oil; it will wilt (and shrink) rather quickly. Cook for about 2 minutes.

Transfer the cooked arugula mixture to the bowl of a food processor. Add the remaining uncooked arugula, red pepper flakes, and walnuts to the food processor, in batches if necessary. Whiz until the mixture becomes an emerald green puree. Add the remaining 1 tablespoon of olive oil and whiz for another minute or so. Add the ½ teaspoon of salt and whiz for a few seconds. Taste, adjust the salt as needed, and add black pepper as you see fit.

Remove the blade from the food processor and measure out 1 cup of the puree. Transfer to a medium-size mixing bowl. (You will have about ¾ cup of leftover puree; store in the fridge in an airtight container and use within 2 days as a sandwich spread, over rice, or devoured with an egg. It's a wonderful cook's treat.)

Rinse out and wipe dry the bowl of the food processor and place the cottage cheese in the bowl. Process until completely blended and smooth; it will look like sour cream. Transfer to the bowl with the arugula puree and stir together until completely integrated. Stir in the nutmeg.

▶ ▶ ▶

- 4 tablespoons olive oil
- 1 small onion, chopped
- 6 cloves garlic, 3 minced and 3 sliced thinly
- 1 medium-size carrot, peeled and minced
- 1 to 2 sprigs fresh oregano or thyme (optional but nice)
- ¼ cup red wine of choice (optional)
- 1 (23- to 28-ounce) container tomato puree (see page 18 for recommendations)
- ½ teaspoon salt, plus more to taste
- Freshly ground black pepper
- 2 bunches arugula, washed thoroughly, stemmed, and spun dry (about 8 cups), or equal amounts of spinach
- ½ teaspoon red pepper flakes (add up to 1 teaspoon if you like heat)
- ¼ cup unsalted walnuts
- ½ cup 2% or full-fat cottage cheese
- ⅛ teaspoon grated nutmeg
- 8 unsalted matzos (less than 1 box)
- 1 cup grated Parmigiano-Reggiano cheese
- 10 to 12 ounces mozzarella cheese, sliced or shredded

TOOLS: *12-inch skillet or wok, food processor, 9 by 13-inch baking dish*

Preheat the oven to 350°F.

Before assembly, it's a good idea to check how the matzos fit inside a 9 by 13-inch baking dish. (Two matzos should easily fit, side by side.) Grease the dish, then wet each matzo under a slow trickle of warm water to moisten. Stack the damp matzos and cover with a damp paper towel.

Spoon enough marinara sauce onto the bottom of the baking dish to cover its surface. Place a layer of matzos side by side, so that they're snug, on top of the sauce. With a rubber spatula, spread half of the arugula filling on top of the matzo, covering the surface, and add one-fourth of the mozzarella and Parmigiano-Reggiano.

Create a new layer of matzo, and this time, spoon in enough marinara sauce to cover the surface, followed by another one-fourth addition of each cheese.

For the third matzo layer, spread the remaining arugula filling on top, followed by another one-fourth addition of each cheese.

For the top layer, place the remaining two matzos, followed by the remaining marinara sauce, spread evenly. Top the whole thing off with the remaining cheese.

Cover with foil and bake the lasagna until fork tender and bubby, about 50 minutes. Remove the foil and allow the cheese to brown for 10 minutes before removing the baking pan from the oven.

MAKES 6 TO 8 SERVINGS

SPRING BREAK PATTY PARTY

As uplifting as the arrival of spring can be, it can also take the wind right out of your sails, if Mother Nature doesn't feel like cooperating. Here in Seattle, spring can be one of the most grueling seasons, a long crawl to summer that can turn the most doe-eyed optimist into a curmudgeon. Getting on an airplane is a fine antidote but not always realistic. Here's where a little countertop travel comes in handy. Using the popular chickpea "crab cake" from *The Meat Lover's Meatless Cookbook* as seasonal base camp, I've come up with three chickpea patty variations with distinctive flavor notes that will transport you to warmer, sunnier spots, even for just a few bites. First stop is Greece, with fresh dill and a feta-yogurt sauce. Before heading home, we make a pit stop in Jamaica, where jerk-seasoned patties await, topped off with a burst of pineapple. Our final stop is the Carolinas—or maybe it's Galveston—where we tuck into Southern-fried chick . . . peas and a barbecue sauce worth sending a postcard about.

- 1 cup dried chickpeas
- 1½ cups finely chopped onion (1 medium-size onion)
- 2 cloves garlic, sliced thinly
- ½ cup fresh dill
- Zest of 1 lemon
- 1 teaspoon dried oregano
- 1 teaspoon salt
- ⅛ teaspoon ground cayenne
- ½ teaspoon baking powder
- ¼ to ½ cup neutral oil
- Feta-yogurt sauce (details follow)
- Garnishes: Sliced cucumber, chopped spinach, pickled peppers, hot sauce

TOOLS: *Food processor or stand blender, parchment paper, 12-inch skillet*

KITCHEN NOTES: *Dried chickpeas are a must for these patties; canned chickpeas are simply too soft.*

GREEK PATTY GF V

A trio of fresh dill, lemon zest, and oregano do a formidable job of inspiring visions of the Acropolis. Wait 'til you taste these patties with a hint of the Feta-Yogurt Sauce.

HERE'S WHAT YOU DO:

Place the beans in a bowl and add enough water to cover by a few inches. Soak for at least 6 hours at room temperature. (If your kitchen is very warm, you may want to place the chickpeas in the refrigerator to minimize the chances of fermentation.) Drain and set aside.

Using a food processor or stand blender, pulverize the chickpeas using the "pulse" function, until the beans form a paste that sticks together when you squeeze it in your hand. Be careful not to overprocess; too smooth, the batter will fall apart when cooking.

Add the remaining ingredients (except the oil) and process, using the "pulse" function about twelve times.

Using a scant ⅓-cup measure, shape the batter into patties and place on a plate. Cover the patties with parchment paper or plastic wrap and refrigerate for at least 30 minutes, or until firm.

Preheat the oven to 350°F.

In a shallow 12-inch skillet, heat ¼ cup of the oil over medium-high heat. Gently place the patties into the hot oil in small batches (don't crowd the pan) and fry the first side until golden brown and slightly crusty, 2 to 3 minutes. Gently turn onto the second side and cook for an additional 2 to 3 minutes. Transfer to a baking tray to finish cooking in the oven until the patties slightly firm up and dry out, about 7 minutes.

To keep the patties warm without further cooking, lower the oven temperature to 225°F.

Serve with a schmear of feta-yogurt sauce and condiments of your choice. These are great as part of a salad or tucked into a soft bun or a toasted pita.

MAKES 7 OR 8 PATTIES

FETA-YOGURT SAUCE

Greek yogurt is the way to go with this sauce; it's thick and creamy and sticks to the bun.

HERE'S WHAT YOU DO:

Pour the yogurt into a small mixing bowl and vigorously stir until creamy. Add the remaining ingredients and blend with an immersion blender or place all the ingredients in a stand blender until well blended. Taste for lemon and salt, and add more as needed.

Keeps in an airtight container in the refrigerator for 2 days.

MAKES ¾ CUP SAUCE. AMOUNTS MAY BE DOUBLED.

- ½ cup 2% or full-fat "traditional" plain Greek yogurt*
- ½ cup feta cheese of choice, drained
- 1 tablespoon freshly squeezed lemon juice, plus more to taste
- 1 to 2 cloves garlic, minced finely
- ½ teaspoon salt
- ¼ teaspoon dried oregano
- Pinch of cayenne

TOOLS: *Immersion or stand blender*

No Greek yogurt to be had? Line a large bowl with a few layers of cheesecloth. Pour the yogurt into the cheesecloth and tie or fasten the ends around the bowl so that the cheesecloth is suspended and can hang. Allow to drain of its water for a few hours.

- 1 cup dried chickpeas
- 1½ cups finely chopped onion (1 medium-size onion)
- ¼ cup scallions, roots and dark green tops removed, chopped
- ½ Scotch bonnet or habanero chile pepper, seeded and minced
- ½ teaspoon baking powder
- 1 teaspoon salt
- 1 teaspoon dried thyme
- 1 teaspoon garlic powder
- ¼ teaspoon ground allspice
- 1 tablespoon curry powder of choice
- ¼ to ½ cup neutral oil

FIXIN'S:

- ½ to ¾ cup prepared jerk sauce
- Pineapple Salsa (page 143)

TOOLS: *Food processor or stand blender, parchment paper, 12-inch skillet*

KITCHEN NOTES: *Dried chickpeas are a must for these patties; canned chickpeas are simply too soft.*

I use commercially prepared jerk sauce as my "ketchup" in this sandwich. Here in the States, Busha Browne and Walkerswood are the two most available brands. Although not jerk-y, Pickapeppa is an excellent stand-in.

JAMAICAN PATTY V

In Jamaica, jerk is a cooking method (slow, over fire, like barbecue) as well as a highly spiced seasoning blend. Although too delicate to be jerked on the grill, this spice-forward patty will take your tongue to the West Indies.

HERE'S WHAT YOU DO:

Place the beans in a bowl and add enough water to cover by a few inches. Soak for at least 6 hours at room temperature. (If your kitchen is very warm, you may want to place the chickpeas in the refrigerator to minimize the chances of fermentation.) Drain and set aside; you now have about 2½ cups of soaked chickpeas.

Using a food processor or stand blender, pulverize the chickpeas using the "pulse" function until the beans form a paste that sticks together when you squeeze it in your hand. Be careful not to overprocess; too smooth and the batter will fall apart when cooking.

Add the remaining ingredients (except the oil) and process, using the "pulse" function about twelve times.

Using a scant ⅓-cup measure, shape the batter into patties and place on a plate. Cover the patties with parchment paper or plastic wrap and refrigerate for at least 30 minutes, or until firm.

Preheat the oven to 350°F.

In a shallow 12-inch skillet, heat ¼ cup of the oil over medium-high heat. Gently place the patties into the hot oil in small batches (don't crowd the pan) and fry the first side until golden brown and slightly crusty, 2 to 3 minutes. Gently turn onto the second side and cook for an additional 2 to 3 minutes. Transfer to a baking tray to finish cooking in the oven, until the patties slightly firm up and dry out, about 7 minutes.

To keep the patties warm without further cooking, lower the oven temperature to 225°F.

Serve by itself or on a bun with jerk sauce, bread-and-butter pickles, 2 tablespoons of pineapple salsa, and/or caramelized onions.

MAKES 7 OR 8 PATTIES.

PINEAPPLE SALSA 🄥

Sweet, yet cooling, this salsa is a dandy patty partner, offsetting the heat of the jerk.

HERE'S WHAT YOU DO:

Place all the ingredients in a medium-size bowl and stir well.

Keeps for 2 days in the refrigerator, but best eaten on the day it is made.

HOW TO CUT UP A PINEAPPLE:

Cut off the bottom to create a flat edge, making the cutting easier and safe, then slice off the top.

From top to bottom, slice away the tough exterior, including the brown prickly things.

Using the core as the focal point, visualize the pineapple as a four-sided object. Place the blade of your knife on the fleshy edge of the core and slice from top to bottom. You should have four large hunks of pineapple, with only the core remaining. Trim away any remaining brown prickly bits and skin.

- 2 cups pineapple, preferably fresh, that has been cut into ½-inch cubes
- Juice of ½ lime
- 1 teaspoon brown sugar
- ¼ cup cilantro leaves, chopped finely
- ¼ teaspoon fresh habanero or Scotch bonnet chile pepper, seeded and minced
- 2 scallions, root and dark tops removed, washed and minced
- ¼ teaspoon salt

SOUTHERN-FRIED CHICK . . . PEA

KIDDO **V**

- 1 cup dried chickpeas
- 1½ cups finely chopped onion (1 medium-size onion)
- ½ teaspoon baking powder
- 1 teaspoon salt
- 1 teaspoon dried oregano
- ½ teaspoon chipotle powder or smoked paprika
- ½ teaspoon ground chile pepper
- 1 teaspoon garlic powder
- ¼ teaspoon fennel seeds
- ¼ teaspoon freshly ground black pepper
- 1 teaspoon brown sugar
- ¼ to ½ cup neutral oil

TOOLS: *Food processor or stand blender, parchment paper, 12-inch skillet*

KITCHEN NOTES: *Dried chickpeas are a must for these patties; canned chickpeas are simply too soft.*

The plan: to create a patty reminiscent of a certain colonel from Kentucky with a secret recipe. For trademark reasons, we couldn't chant, "Gimme a K, gimme an F, gimme a C," but I think you'll agree, this patty is as chick-licious as it gets.

HERE'S WHAT YOU DO:

Place the beans in a bowl and add enough water to cover by a few inches. Soak for at least 6 hours at room temperature. (If your kitchen is very warm, you may want to place the chickpeas in the refrigerator to minimize the chances of fermentation.)

Drain and set aside; you now have about 2½ cups of soaked chickpeas.

Using a food processor or stand blender, pulverize the chickpeas using the "pulse" function, until the beans form a paste that sticks together when you squeeze it in your hand. Be careful not to overprocess; too smooth and the batter will fall apart when cooking.

Add the remaining ingredients (except the oil) and process, using the "pulse" function about twelve times.

Using a scant ⅓-cup measure, shape the batter into patties and place on a plate. Cover the patties with parchment paper or plastic wrap and refrigerate for at least 30 minutes, or until firm.

Preheat the oven to 350°F.

In a shallow 12-inch skillet, heat ¼ cup of the oil over medium-high heat. Gently place the patties into the hot oil in small batches (don't crowd the pan) and fry the first side until golden brown and slightly crusty, 2 to 3 minutes. Gently turn onto the second side and cook for an additional 2 to 3 minutes. Transfer to a baking tray to finish cooking in the oven until the patties slightly firm up and dry out, about 7 minutes.

To keep the patties warm without further cooking, lower the oven temperature to 225°F.

Warm the barbecue sauce (page 147) and brush some on each side of the patties. Serve by itself or on a bun with extra sauce, or caramelized onions (page 146).

MAKES 7 OR 8 PATTIES

CARAMELIZED ONIONS

- 2 to 3 tablespoons olive oil or butter

- 2 cups onion that have been sliced into half-moons (not quite 1 large onion)

TOOLS: *10- or 12-inch skillet*

HERE'S WHAT YOU DO:

In a 10- or 12-inch skillet, heat the oil or melt the butter over medium heat and add the onion. Cook over medium-low heat, stirring every 5 minutes, adjusting the heat to ensure that the onion is cooking evenly and not burning. Gradually the onion will soften, shrink, and sweeten, becoming caramelized in about 45 minutes.

Caramelized onions keep in the refrigerator in an airtight container for up to 5 days.

MAKES ABOUT ¾ CUP CARAMELIZED ONIONS. AMOUNTS MAY BE DOUBLED OR TRIPLED.

FINGER-LICKING BARBECUE SAUCE `KIDDO`

The addition of the butter is borrowed from cookbook author and grill guru Dave Joachim, who's right; it really cranks up the umami in this sauce. Tester Jen Hicks says that she will never buy jarred barbecue sauce again.

HERE'S WHAT YOU DO:

Place all the ingredients into a small saucepan and stir until thoroughly mixed, over medium heat. Bring to a boil and then lower the heat to low, stirring to minimize burning. The sauce is ready when it is heated through. Take off the heat until ready to use.

Keeps in an airtight container in the refrigerator for about 1 week.

MAKES ABOUT 1½ CUPS. AMOUNTS MAY BE DOUBLED.

- 1 cup ketchup, preferably organic
- 1 tablespoon brown sugar
- 1 tablespoon yellow mustard
- 1 tablespoon cider vinegar
- 1 tablespoon Worcestershire sauce (Anchovy-free Plan B: Pickapeppa sauce)
- 1 tablespoon unsulfured molasses
- 1 tablespoon honey
- 1 teaspoon chipotle powder or smoked paprika
- ½ teaspoon garlic powder
- ½ teaspoon onion powder
- ¼ teaspoon freshly ground black pepper
- ½ teaspoon salt
- 1 tablespoon butter (optional but delightful)

JICAMA SALAD   KIDDO V

- 4 cups jicama that has been peeled and cut into ¼-inch matchsticks (about 1 pound)
- ¼ teaspoon cayenne or ground chile pepper of choice
- ½ teaspoon salt
- Zest of 1 lime, plus juice of ½ lime
- 1 tablespoon olive oil
- Pinch of sugar
- 1 medium-size orange (spring and summer option: ½ cup strawberries)
- ½ cup fresh cilantro leaves, chopped finely

Until trying this recipe, tester Jules Cechony had never used jicama in her own kitchen and wondered why she waited so long. Jicama is a root vegetable with a somewhat thick but peelable skin. It is loaded with vitamin C and just 50 calories per cup—with a satisfying crunch that is a great distraction from chips.

HERE'S WHAT YOU DO:

Place the jicama in a large bowl. Add the chile pepper, salt, lime zest and juice, olive oil, and sugar and mix everything together until the jicama is evenly coated with the seasonings.

Peel the orange and slice off the top and bottom edges to make the fruit flat against your work surface. Remove any white pith, then slice between the membranes, resulting in segments. Remove any seeds as necessary. If strawberries are in season, remove the stems and slice into quarters.

Toss in the fruit (squeeze any remaining orange juice) and top the salad with the cilantro.

Eat immediately.

MAKES 6 SERVINGS

RHUBARB BUCKLE

A simple vanilla-scented batter is topped with seasonal fruit and crowned with a brown sugar crumb. As the cake layer rises, the fruit topping sinks (or "buckles"), hence the name. This recipe re-appears on the Father's Day menu, with blueberries as the main attraction.

HERE'S WHAT YOU DO:

Make the topping: In a small bowl, stir together ¼ cup of the flour, the brown sugar, and the cinnamon. Measure out 2 tablespoons of the butter, and cut into small dice. Work the butter into the flour mixture with your fingertips until the butter is integrated. Cover and refrigerate.

Bring the water to a boil in a medium-size saucepan. Add the rhubarb, return to a boil, and cook for 2 minutes over medium-high heat. Strain and run under cold running water. Set aside.

Preheat the oven to 350°F. Grease an 8- or 9-inch square baking dish.

In a small bowl, place the remaining ¾ cup of the flour, the baking powder, and the salt, and stir together.

Cut the remaining 4 tablespoons of butter into tablespoon-size pieces. In the bowl of a stand mixer or using a handheld electric mixer, cream the butter and the granulated sugar until well blended and fluffy. Add the egg and mix until well blended, followed by the vanilla. It may look a little curdled and that's okay.

Add the dry ingredients to the wet, alternating with the milk, mixing until smooth and blended. Note: I like to use the electric beater for the first addition, then finish mixing the batter by hand with a rubber spatula.

Pour the batter into the prepared pan and spread so that it evenly covers the pan. Cover the batter with the fruit, followed by the topping, which should cover the entire surface.

Bake for 40 minutes, or until the topping is golden brown.

Allow to cool slightly in the pan and serve warm or at room temperature.

MAKES ABOUT 6 SERVINGS

- 1 cup all-purpose flour
- ¼ cup light or dark brown sugar
- ½ teaspoon ground cinnamon
- 6 tablespoons butter, plus more for greasing the baking dish
- 4 cups water
- 2 cups rhubarb that has had its leaves removed, washed and cut into ½-inch-thick slices
- 1½ teaspoons baking powder
- ¼ teaspoon salt
- ½ cup granulated sugar
- 1 egg, beaten lightly
- 1 teaspoon vanilla extract
- ¼ cup milk of choice (I have used coconut and cow's milk with equal success)

TOOLS: 8- or 9-inch square baking dish, stand or handheld mixer

KITCHEN NOTES: Be sure to remove the leaves from rhubarb stalks, as they are poisonous. The stalks will need a quick dip in boiling water to coax them into stewy morsels. Here, the rhubarb goes solo, which can be a tad sour for some; feel free to use half the amount and pair up with 1 cup of thinly sliced strawberries.

SALUTING MOM AND DAD

For much of my adult life, I've harbored a fantasy that my father, who died when I was just sixteen, would come back for just one night and have dinner with me. In the '70s, when he wore platform shoes, he'd make an occasional appearance in the kitchen, wowing me and my younger brothers with chocolate milk shakes and French fries painstakingly hand cut from russet potatoes. I thought about him as I tested the fries made from chickpea flour and shaped two kinds of black beans into patties that could have changed his tune about his beloved Brontosaurus burgers.

With the rug pulled from underneath her, my mother carried the torch and raised us, as she tried to get our inherited cholesterol levels under control. The kitchen of my youth was more *Pee-wee's Playhouse* than *Better Homes & Gardens*. Hanging on the walls were found objects from her weekly garage sale adventures. The countertops were prime real estate for Americana rather than cutting boards; next to the toaster was a vintage mint green milk shake maker, the kind you'd see in a diner. The dining room was pink, yellow, and green, not unlike an Easter egg.

Susan loves being waited on, especially at the table. The menu is my thank-you note (a form of etiquette she insisted we learn from an early age) to her, a spread that includes one of her all-time favorite vegetables, roasted spears of "asparagris" all dressed up with a cloak of pulverized almonds. She'll dine on "creamed" spinach seasoned with ginger and coconut milk, a departure from the bowl she once dumped on my father's head in the heat of an argument. I'll ask her to dig out some parfait glasses (from another era, natch) to fill with sweetened whipped Greek yogurt and stewed rhubarb, a tribute to her grandmother, who raised her.

CHICKPEA CREPES WITH ZESTY MASHED POTATOES AND INDIAN-SPICED SPINACH SAUCE GF V

This dish is part of a three-ring circus, but everything can be made in a staggered fashion and reheated when ready to serve. Make the filling and sauce before the crepes.

Chickpea flour tends to clump up; do your best to whisk it away with a fork, but don't fret if some clumps remain. The crepes may be made an hour or so in advance and can be kept or gently reheated in a low oven, covered with foil until ready to use.

ZESTY MASHED POTATOES

The potatoes do not need to be completely peeled, just where there are boo-boos and dings. Fresh chile pepper is preferred; if you can't get it, don't worry.

HERE'S WHAT YOU DO:

Cut the potatoes into quarters or eighths (depending on the size). Place in a medium-size saucepan fitted with a lid along with the water, 2 teaspoons of the salt, and the garlic. The water should just cover the potatoes. Cover the saucepan and bring to a boil. Lower the heat to medium and cook the potatoes for 25 minutes, or until fork tender.

With a slotted spoon or spider strainer, remove the potatoes and reserve the cooking water. Transfer the potatoes to a mixing bowl, and with a hand masher, mash the potatoes.

Gradually ladle in some of the cooking water to moisten the potatoes; be sure to do this incrementally to avoid a soupy mess. You may also drizzle in some olive oil for lubrication, but the cooking water is usually adequate. Add the chile pepper, ginger, and cilantro, and stir to incorporate. Taste and add a few squeezes of the lime half to wake up the mixture, and add the remaining ½ teaspoon of salt, if needed.

Cover the potatoes with foil to keep warm while you assemble the rest of the dish.

▶ ▶ ▶

ZESTY MASHED POTATOES:

- 2 pounds russet potatoes or medium-starch varieties (Yellow Finn or Yukon Gold), scrubbed, trimmed of bruises or eyes, peeled as needed (about 5 medium-size potatoes)
- 4 cups water
- 2½ teaspoons salt
- 2 cloves garlic, peeled
- Olive oil (optional)
- ¾ to 1 teaspoon fresh chile pepper of choice, seeded and minced
- 1½ teaspoons peeled and very finely minced fresh ginger (a piece about 2 by 1-inch)
- ⅓ cup fresh cilantro, washed, dried, and chopped finely
- ½ lime, for seasoning

TOOLS: *Handheld potato masher, slotted spoon or spider strainer*

INDIAN-SPICED SPINACH SAUCE:

- 3 cloves garlic, sliced

- 1 heaping teaspoon thinly sliced fresh ginger

- ¼ to ¾ teaspoon seeded and minced fresh chile pepper of choice, to taste

- ⅓ cup water

- 1½ tablespoons neutral oil

- 1 tablespoon curry powder of choice

- 10 cups washed and chopped spinach (about 1¼ pounds spinach)

- ½ teaspoon salt, plus more to taste

- ⅓ to ½ cup coconut milk

- ½ lime, for seasoning

TOOLS: *Mortar and pestle, 12-inch skillet, stand blender or food processor*

No mortar and pestle? Slice the garlic and lay the flat side of a chef's knife on top. With one hand on the handle and the palm of your other hand on top of the knife, press on the garlic in a smearing fashion. Repeat with the ginger.

INDIAN-SPICED SPINACH SAUCE

HERE'S WHAT YOU DO:

Using a mortar and pestle,* pulverize the garlic and ginger into a paste. Place the garlic, ginger, and chile pepper in a small bowl with the water and stir.

Get a 12-inch skillet hot over medium-high heat and swirl in the oil. Pour in the garlic mixture and stir. The reaction will be noisy, and that's okay. Stir the mixture for about 30 seconds, then stir in the curry powder. The mixture will be pasty. Add the spinach in small batches, turning with tongs to coat with the spices and oil. The spinach will wilt quickly and shrink substantially. Season with the salt and taste.

Transfer the mixture to a stand blender or a food processor and puree, being mindful of the hot splattering liquid.

Pour the puree into a small saucepan and warm over medium heat. Add ⅓ cup of the coconut milk, adding more as needed to loosen up the sauce, and season with lime, to taste, plus more salt if needed.

CHICKPEA CREPES

To flip these delicate crepes, use a thin-edged turner or spatula made from wood or bamboo. A silicone or metal turner is too bulky.

HERE'S WHAT YOU DO:

In a medium-size bowl, combine all the ingredients (except for the oil) in a medium bowl, whisking until the batter is well blended and as lump-free as possible.

Let the batter settle for about 15 minutes.

Over medium-high heat, get the 8-inch nonstick skillet very hot; you can test it by adding a bead of water, which should vaporize upon contact.

Brush the skillet with oil, then cook the crepes one by one, using a ¼-cup measure for the batter. Tilt the skillet to ensure that the batter completely covers the surface. Lower the heat to medium and cook until bubbles appear in the middle of the crepe, about 90 seconds.

Flip onto the second side and cook for an additional 90 seconds. The crepe will be lightly golden when done. Transfer to a plate, cover with a towel to keep warm, and continue with the rest of the batter, brushing the skillet with oil each time.

You may hold crepes in a 225°F oven, covered with foil.

ASSEMBLING THE CREPES:

Spoon ¼ cup of the mashed potatoes on one-half of each crepe. Use a spoon to spread the filling evenly. Fold the crepes over to close. Ladle ⅛ cup of warm spinach sauce over each crepe. Serve hot.

2 CREPES PER SERVING

CHICKPEA CREPES:

- 2 cups chickpea flour
- 2 cups water
- 1 teaspoon salt
- 2 tablespoons cornstarch or arrowroot powder
- Neutral oil, for brushing

TOOLS: *Balloon whisk, 8-inch nonstick skillet, wooden or bamboo turner with a thin edge*

ROASTED ASPARAGUS WITH GREMOLATA AND ALMOND STAR DUST **V** **GF**

Gremolata is a mixture of parsley, lemon zest, and garlic traditionally used as a garnish for osso buco, but there's no reason we have to wait until veal shank night to enjoy this herbal breath of freshness. The "star dust" adds yet another layer of flavor, texture, and (monounsaturated) fat—almonds, by the way, are a nutritional powerhouse, loaded with calcium, vitamin E, magnesium and protein.

HERE'S WHAT YOU DO:

Place the asparagus in a large bowl and add the olive oil and salt, tossing until completely coated.

Preheat the oven to 400°F.

Transfer the asparagus to two baking sheets, arranged in a single layer. Roast for 8 minutes and check for doneness. Note: Very fresh, just-picked asparagus often cooks quickly. Cook in 3-minute increments until the asparagus is as tender as you like it.

While the asparagus roasts, place the parsley, garlic, and half of the lemon zest in a small bowl and stir together.

Pulverize the almonds in a clean coffee grinder or stand blender. You're looking for some flecks of texture; pieces of the nuts are okay.

Place the asparagus in a serving dish or shallow bowl. Sprinkle the gremolata all over the asparagus, followed by the "dust."

Eat hot or at room temperature.

MAKES 6 SERVINGS

- 2 bunches asparagus, woody ends removed (about 20 stalks)
- 2 tablespoons olive oil
- ½ teaspoon salt
- ½ cup fresh flat-leaf parsley leaves, chopped finely
- 1 clove garlic, minced finely
- Zest of 2 lemons
- ¼ cup unsalted whole roasted almonds

TOOLS: *Coffee grinder or stand blender*

RHUBARB-STRAWBERRY FOOL
GF **KIDDO**

- 1¼ pounds rhubarb, trimmed of leaves, chopped into ½-inch pieces (4 to 5 medium-size stalks rhubarb), or 4 cups frozen rhubarb

- ⅓ cup honey

- ⅛ cup water

- 2 tablespoons pomegranate molasses (optional but nice)

- ¼ teaspoon freshly squeezed lemon juice (a slight squeeze of ½ lemon)

- 1½ cups 2% or "traditional" full-fat plain Greek yogurt

- ⅓ cup confectioners' sugar, plus more to taste

- 12 to 15 strawberries, hulled and sliced thinly

- Fresh mint or basil leaves, for garnish (optional)

TOOLS: *Balloon whisk*

KITCHEN NOTES: *The rhubarb can be made ahead and refrigerated overnight, and the entire dish can be assembled a few hours in advance and refrigerated until ready to serve. Eight-ounce canning jars make terrific stand-ins for parfait glasses, and their accompanying lids earn them major porta-picnic points.*

The name comes from the French word *fouler*, which means to mash. And that's what a fool is—mashed-up fruit, sitting pretty in a parfait glass. Here, I've paired strawberries with stewed rhubarb (botanically not a fruit, by the way), which, when finished off with a smidge of pomegranate molasses, is dreamy. In lieu of whipped cream, I layer the fruit with plain Greek yogurt that miraculously whips into pillowy loveliness.

HERE'S WHAT YOU DO:

In a medium-size saucepan, combine the rhubarb, honey, and water and bring to a boil. Cover and cook over medium heat, stirring occasionally, until the rhubarb breaks down, 10 to 15 minutes.

Uncover and cook, stirring often, until the liquid has evaporated and the rhubarb is thick and jammy, an additional 10 minutes. Transfer the rhubarb to a bowl and refrigerate until chilled through.

Meanwhile, place the yogurt into a medium-size bowl, along with the confectioners' sugar, and whisk vigorously. The yogurt will loosen and whip quite readily. Taste for sweetness, and add more sugar as needed.

When ready to assemble, add the pomegranate molasses (if using) to the chilled rhubarb, as well as the lemon juice, and stir well.

Spoon ⅛ cup of the rhubarb into the bottom of six wine or parfait glasses. Layer with one sliced strawberry and ⅛ cup of the whipped yogurt. Repeat with an additional ⅛ cup of rhubarb, followed by one sliced strawberry and a topping of ⅛ cup of whipped yogurt.

Garnish with additional strawberry slices and/or mint or basil.

MAKES 6 SERVINGS

CHICKPEA FRIES   V GF KIDDO

How in the world does chickpea flour cooked on top of the stove like polenta morph into a batch of fries? Very simply, I'm pleased to report. Better still, these crispy fries are just as savory as the potato variety. After months of testing, I'm still wowed. Fun date night snack, DVD munchies, or school break activity.

HERE'S WHAT YOU DO:

Line a baking sheet with parchment paper.

Bring the water to a boil in a large saucepan. Gradually (and carefully—hot alert!) add the chickpea flour, whisking to eliminate lumps (but don't fret if you don't get them all), followed by the oregano, garlic powder, salt, chile pepper, olive oil, and black pepper.

Lower the heat to medium-low and cook for about 5 minutes, stirring to minimize sticking. The mixture will be thick and bubbly, resembling polenta.

Carefully pour the hot mixture onto the prepared pan, spreading evenly to completely fill the pan. Cover with plastic wrap and cool for about 15 minutes. Then transfer to the refrigerator to chill and firm, about 1 hour. (This step can be done a day in advance.)

When ready to fry, pour the oil in a deep saucepan or wok and heat to 350°F. (Use the candy thermometer to keep an eye on the temperature.) Arrange a few paper towels on an adjacent work surface to drain the fries after they've been fried.

Cut the batter into 3- or 4-inch-long fries or another similarly sized shape that makes you happy. Dip the shapes in the hot oil in small batches and fry until golden and slightly puffy, about 4 minutes.

Remove with a slotted spoon or spider strainer and transfer to the paper towel–lined area. Season with salt to taste while hot.

Return the oil to 350°F before frying subsequent batches.

Serve with ketchup, Kicky Ketchup (page 39), or Finger-Licking Barbecue Sauce (page 147). Best served right after they've been made.

MAKES AT LEAST 6 SERVINGS

- 4 cups water
- 2 cups chickpea flour
- 1 teaspoon dried oregano
- 1 teaspoon garlic powder
- 1 teaspoon salt, plus more to taste
- ¼ teaspoon cayenne or ground chile pepper of choice
- 2 tablespoons olive oil
- Freshly ground black pepper
- 2 cups neutral oil

TOOLS: *Parchment paper, candy thermometer, slotted spoon or spider strainer*

DOUBLE BLACK BEAN BURGERS

I use two kinds of black beans here—the turtle beans so often found in chili and burritos, plus fermented soybeans (details on page 8) from the Chinese pantry. Just a little dab of these pungent salty morsels will transform an ordinary bean patty into a burger with kapow.

HERE'S WHAT YOU DO:

Place the turtle beans in a bowl and cover with about 3 inches of water. Soak for at least 4 hours. (In warmer climes, soak the beans in the refrigerator to avoid sprouting or fermentation.)

Drain the beans. Transfer to a medium-size or large pot fitted with a lid and cover with about 4 cups of water; you're looking for at least 2 inches of water above the beans. Add the garlic and bring to a boil. Cook at a hard boil for 5 minutes. Cover, lower the heat, and cook at a gentle simmer. At minute 20, stir in ½ teaspoon of the salt. At minute 45, check the beans for doneness. Cook in 10-minute increments until the beans are tender to the bite, keeping in mind that cooking times may vary, depending on the age of the beans.

While the turtle beans cook, soak the fermented black beans in 1 tablespoon of water for about 20 minutes. Drain, mince, and set aside.

Measure out ¼ cup of the turtle beans, using a slotted spoon to drain, and reserve. Using a slotted spoon or spider sieve to drain, transfer the remaining turtle beans to a medium-size bowl. With a handheld potato masher, mash the beans into a paste, allowing for a small amount of texture.

Stir in the fermented black beans, scallions, ginger, and sesame oil. Taste, and add the remaining ¼ teaspoon salt if needed. Add the rice flour, chile pepper, egg, and the reserved ¼ cup of turtle beans. The mixture will come together almost like a dough. It will be slightly sticky.

Make patties using a ¼-cup measure; you'll end up with six patties. While shaping, think burger, rather than meatball. Cover with parchment paper or plastic and refrigerate for about 30 minutes.

- ¾ cup dried black turtle beans
- 1 clove garlic, peeled and left whole
- ½ to ¾ teaspoon salt
- 1 tablespoon fermented black beans
- ¼ cup scallions, roots and dark green part removed, minced
- 1 teaspoon peeled and minced fresh ginger
- 1 teaspoon sesame oil
- 6 tablespoons white rice flour (not to be confused with sweet rice flour)
- ½ teaspoon ground chile pepper of choice
- 1 egg, beaten
- ¼ to ½ cup neutral oil
- 6 soft hamburger buns or English muffins, toasted
- Possible fixin's: Plain spreadable goat cheese, roasted peppers, pickled peppers, romaine lettuce, or arugula

TOOLS: *Parchment paper, slotted spoon or spider strainer, handheld potato masher*

Preheat the oven to 350°F.

To panfry: Heat ¼ cup of the oil in a 9- or 10-inch skillet over medium-high heat. In batches of three, cook the patties until golden brown, about 3 minutes per side. Feel free to gently flatten with a spatula to shape into a patty. Add more oil as needed, and heat before adding more patties. Transfer to a baking sheet and finish cooking all of the patties in the oven for an additional 7 minutes.

To grill: Grease the grates while preheating. Brush the patties liberally on both sides with ¼ cup of the oil, using more as needed.

When the grill arrives at 350°F, cook over direct heat until golden brown on each side, 3 to 4 minutes per side. To finish cooking, transfer to the oven or move the patties away from the direct heat and cook for an additional 6 to 7 minutes.

Serve on a bun of your choice (I'm a big fan of book-ending my patties with a whole wheat English muffin) and with any of the suggested fixin's.

MAKES 6 SERVINGS

KITCHEN NOTES: *Asian markets are where you'll find fermented black beans, often packaged in vacuum-style bags and labeled as salted black beans or dow see (the Cantonese word). Do not substitute prepared black bean–garlic sauce.*

Rice flour is available both at Asian markets and in conventional and specialty supermarkets, where you may see Bob's Red Mill packages.

While the turtle beans cook, you can do the prep for seasoning the patties to save some time.

These patties are sturdy and can be either panfried or grilled, but the former yields more of a crust.

CAESAR-Y SALAD WITH TOFU CROUTONS Ⓥ

In my quest to develop a Caesar salad that all eaters could dig into, I left behind the egg, anchovies, and Worcestershire sauce of the time-honored version and swapped in briny capers and umami-rich molasses (as well as a smidge of soy sauce). I don't think you'll miss a thing.

HERE'S WHAT YOU DO:

Drain the tofu: Remove from the package and place on a dinner plate. Place a second plate on top of the tofu and weigh it down with a filled can or jar. Allow to sit for about 20 minutes.

Meanwhile, tear the romaine into bite-size pieces and place in a large salad bowl.

Preheat the oven to 450°F, and line a baking sheet with parchment paper.

Drain off the water from the tofu. Slice the tofu in half crosswise. Cut each half into sixteen to twenty 1-inch cubes (for a total of thirty-two to forty cubes). Transfer the tofu cubes to a mixing bowl, add the neutral oil and the salt, and with your hands, gently mix until the tofu is evenly coated and seasoned.

Arrange the tofu in a single layer on the prepared pan, with a fingernail's distance in between cubes.

Roast for 15 minutes, then with tongs, turn the cubes to brown on a second side. Roast for an additional 15 minutes. The tofu will be golden and slightly puffy.

While the tofu roasts, make the vinaigrette: Using a mortar and pestle,* pulverize the garlic, along with a pinch of salt, into a paste. Add the capers and smash until blended.

Transfer the garlic mash to a small bowl. Add the lemon juice, mustard, molasses, and soy sauce, and whisk together with a fork until well blended. While whisking, gradually add the olive oil until well blended. Taste for oil/acid balance, and adjust as needed.

▶ ▶ ▶

- 1 (14-ounce) package fresh extra-firm tofu, preferably organic
- 1½ bunches romaine lettuce, washed thoroughly, dried and trimmed (about 12 cups)
- 2 tablespoons neutral oil
- 1 teaspoon salt, plus more for pulverizing garlic
- 3 to 4 cloves garlic, peeled and sliced
- ¾ teaspoon capers
- Juice of 1½ lemons (about 6 tablespoons)
- 1½ teaspoons Dijon mustard
- 1½ teaspoons unsulfured molasses
- 1½ teaspoons soy sauce, *shoyu*, or wheat-free tamari
- ⅓ cup olive oil
- About ½ cup grated Parmigiano-Reggiano cheese, plus more to taste, for garnish (optional)

TOOLS: *Parchment paper, mortar and pestle*

*No mortar and pestle? Slice the garlic and lay the flat side of a chef's knife on top. With one hand on the handle (which is close to you, off the edge of cutting surface) and the palm of your other hand on top of the knife, press on the garlic in a smearing fashion, followed by the capers.

This salad can work equally well as a side or an entrée, particularly with the protein-packed tofu croutons. The amounts below will make a big, family-style salad, enough for six hearty helpings. If there are just a few of you, you may reduce the amounts by one-third. Keep the tofu proportions just as they are; the croutons make great leftovers and keep well for a few days. Leftover vinaigrette will maintain its lemony punch for a day or two in the refrigerator; without the raw egg, there's less worry, too. I love that romaine lettuce is packed with nutrients, but did you know that it's a good source of calcium and heart-healthy omega-3 fatty acids?

Plan B: Place everything in an 8-ounce jar, seal with lid, and shake the vinaigrette like crazy until well blended.

Transfer the roasted tofu to a bowl. Measure out ¼ cup of the vinaigrette and pour over the tofu, gently tossing to coat.

Pour half of the remaining vinaigrette over the romaine and toss with tongs until the leaves are well coated. Add more vinaigrette as needed, being careful not to overdress. Stir in the seasoned tofu cubes and add the grated cheese if using.

MAKES 6 SERVINGS

BLUEBERRY BUCKLE `KIDDO`

Sound familiar? This recipe also appears in the Spring Break Patty Party menu (page 139), with rhubarb as the main attraction. If blueberries fail to call your name, feel free to swap them out with raspberries, blackberries—or if you live in the Pacific Northwest, marionberries!

HERE'S WHAT YOU DO:

Make the topping: In a small bowl, stir together ¼ cup of the flour, the brown sugar, and the cinnamon. Measure out 2 tablespoons of the butter, and cut into small dice. Work the butter into the flour mixture with your fingertips until the butter is integrated and there are no loose bits. Cover and refrigerate while you prepare the batter.

Preheat the oven to 350°F. Grease an 8- or 9-inch square baking dish.

In a small bowl, combine the remaining ¾ cup of flour, the baking powder, and the salt, and stir together.

Cut the remaining 4 tablespoons of butter into tablespoon-size pieces. In the bowl of a stand mixer or using a handheld electric mixer, cream the butter and the granulated sugar until well blended and fluffy. Add the egg and mix until well blended, followed by the vanilla. It may look a little curdled and that's okay.

Add the dry ingredients to the wet, alternating with the milk, mixing until smooth and blended. Note: I like to use the electric beater for the first addition, then finish mixing the batter by hand with a rubber spatula.

Pour the batter into the prepared pan and spread with a rubber spatula so that it evenly covers the pan. Cover the batter with the berries, followed by the topping, which should cover the entire surface.

Bake for 40 minutes, or until the topping is golden brown.

Allow to cool slightly in the pan and serve warm or at room temperature.

MAKES ABOUT 6 SERVINGS

- 1 cup all-purpose flour
- ¼ cup light or dark brown sugar
- ½ teaspoon ground cinnamon
- 6 tablespoons butter, plus more for greasing the baking dish
- 1½ teaspoons baking powder
- ¼ teaspoon salt
- ½ cup granulated sugar
- 1 egg, beaten lightly
- 1 teaspoon vanilla extract
- ¼ cup milk of choice (I have used coconut and cow's milk with equal success)
- 1½ cups blueberries, washed

TOOLS: *8- or 9-inch square baking dish, stand mixer or handheld electric mixer*

CINCO DE MAYO

North of the Mexico border, the fifth of May has long been confused with that country's Independence Day (which is September 16). In fact, it's more of a regional commemoration of the Battle of Puebla in 1862, when Mexico defeated French forces. Historic relevance aside, it's a great excuse to explore a rich culinary heritage little known to Americans beyond tacos and burritos. We celebrate with *sopes*, palm-size griddled tartlets made from masa harina that make terrific containers for *frijoles negros*, black beans that I've seasoned with an umami-rich *sofrito*. Just looking at the filled *sopes* makes me happy, as they're festive without being fussy. The chocolate pudding will stop you in your tracks, as you just won't believe something so creamy is made from tofu.

SANDRA'S SOPES   V GF KIDDO

In the summer of 2011, I spent a weekend cooking with five dynamic women all working in some facet of the culinary world. We cooked as if it were our last day on earth. One of the most memorable dishes was the *sopes* from Sandra Gutierrez, author of *The New Southern-Latino Table*. Sandra, who's also a walking encyclopedia of the culinary history of Latin America, guided me on my maiden voyage with masa harina, the same flour used to make corn tortillas. The masa is shaped into tartlets, fried or griddled, and then filled with savory morsels. With her blessing, I'm sharing Sandra's way of making *sopes*, filled with my version of black beans seasoned with *sofrito*, a vegetable and herb puree that is the foundation of Latin American cookery.

HERE'S WHAT YOU DO:

Sofrito-Seasoned Black Beans

Soak and cook the beans: Place 1 cup of dried black beans in a bowl and cover with about 3 inches of water. Soak for at least 4 hours. (In warmer climes, soak the beans in the refrigerator to avoid sprouting or fermentation.)

Drain the beans. Transfer to a medium-size or large pot fitted with a lid and cover with about 7 cups of water; you're looking for at least 2 inches of water above the beans. Add the garlic and bring to a boil. Cook at a hard boil for 5 minutes. Cover, lower the heat, and cook at a gentle simmer. At minute 20, stir in ½ teaspoon of the salt. At minute 45, check the beans for doneness. Cook in 10-minute increments until the beans are tender to the bite, keeping in mind that cooking times may vary, depending on the age of the beans. On average, they should be tender in about 75 minutes. Drain the beans but reserve their liquid.

While the beans are cooking, make the *sofrito*: In the bowl of a stand blender or food processor, puree the peppers, onion, and remaining six cloves of garlic, followed by the cilantro. Pureeing the ingredients in

▶ ▶ ▶

SOFRITO-SEASONED BLACK BEANS:

- 3 cups cooked black beans (from 1 cup soaked beans or two 15-ounce cans)

- 7 cloves garlic, 1 left whole, the rest smashed

- ¾ to 1 teaspoon salt

- ¾ pound mild or sweet peppers (bell, cubanelle, Anaheim), chopped roughly

- ½ large or 1 small jalapeño chile pepper, seeded and chopped (for hotter results, use a serrano chile pepper)

- ¾ cup onion, chopped (½ medium-size onion)

- 1½ cups fresh cilantro leaves, washed and dried

- 1 Roma tomato

- 1 tablespoon dried oregano

- 6 tablespoons olive oil

TOOLS: *Food processor or stand blender, 12-inch skillet*

KITCHEN NOTES: *Onion, garlic, and sweet peppers are the basis of a sofrito, but each country in Latin America imparts its own spin on the theme. In Mexico, tomato is part of the mix, as is the heat of a jalapeño or serrano chile pepper.*

You may use canned beans in a pinch, but hands down, soaking and cooking your own beans is the more flavorful and texturally interesting option.

SOPES:

- 2 cups masa harina (also sold as instant masa harina)

- ¼ teaspoon plus ⅛ teaspoon salt

- 1½ cups warm water

- Neutral oil, for brushing

- Suggested toppings and garnishes: Sliced avocado, cotija cheese, pico de gallo (details follow), or pineapple salsa (page 143)

TOOLS: *Tortilla press, griddle, or flat-topped grill pan, 5-inch dough scraper*

stages helps ensure a smoother puree. Add the tomato, oregano, and 2 tablespoons of the olive oil and blend until you have a mixture that resembles a pesto.

You'll have a total of 2¾ cups of *sofrito*. Measure out ⅔ cup for the beans. The rest can be poured into ice cube trays and frozen and used for another time. (One ice cube equals 2 tablespoons.)

Place a 12-inch skillet over medium-high heat and swirl in the remaining 4 tablespoons of olive oil, coating the surface of the pan. Add the ⅔ cup of *sofrito* and sauté, stirring regularly, until it becomes thicker and pastier (a sign that the water content is evaporating).

Add the drained beans (or the contents of two cans), and stir until well coated with the *sofrito*. Add enough bean cooking liquid (or water) for it to just meet the level of the beans. Allow the mixture to come to a boil, then lower the heat and cook at a simmer, until the liquid reduces slightly and the mixture thickens, about 30 minutes. Taste for salt, and add the remaining ½ teaspoon salt in increments, tasting along the way.

Keep off the heat until ready to fill the *sopes* and gently reheat.

Sopes

Stir together the masa harina and salt in a large bowl. While stirring, gradually add the water; the dough will form into a ball and should be pliable rather than crumbly. Cover the dough with a damp towel for 10 minutes.

Line both sides of a tortilla press with plastic wrap.

Scoop the dough out of the bowl and cut into twelve to sixteen equal parts. Roll each piece of dough into a ball and keep covered as you work.

One by one, place a dough ball in the center of the bottom plate of the tortilla press. The top plate will follow. Press down the metal lever; the dough will be a flattened into a 4-inch round, about ⅓-inch thick.

With the help of the dough scraper, lift the dough round off the plastic and transfer to a work surface. With your fingers, make a raised edge all around, shaping the round into a tartlet. You want to create a well in the middle so it can be filled.

Heat a griddle or the flat side of a grill pan over high heat and generously brush with the oil. Working in small batches, gently place the

▶ ▶ ▶

KITCHEN NOTES: *The beans can be made in advance and reheated when ready to serve. The masa is best mixed just before cooking, as it continues to absorb water and dry out as it sits. The sopes, too, are best made just before serving; in a pinch, you can keep them covered in the oven at 250°F, but over time, they get tough. Masa harina is available in Latin markets but also in many conventional supermarkets. Sandra's pick is Maseca brand. As a side note, most masa is made from GE (genetically engineered) corn; Bob's Red Mill is one of the few commercially available brands offering non-GMO masa.*

A tortilla press is recommended but it's not a deal breaker, says Sandra. "You can use a plastic bag and heavy skillet. Place a ball of masa in the bag, then press it down with the skillet in place of the tortilla press." Look for tortilla presses in Latin markets or online.

sopes onto the hot pan and brush the tops and sides with oil. Cook for 3 to 4 minutes per side, adjusting the heat to avoid premature browning or burning. The *sopes* will have little char marks and will dry out, revealing dough specks.

Fill each *sope* with ¼ cup of the reheated beans, and garnish with toppings of your choice.

MAKES 6 TO 8 SERVINGS

PICO DE GALLO   `KIDDO` `V`

Translated literally as "rooster's beak," pico de gallo is the fresh tomato salsa that is a staple condiment of Mexican cookery. A snap to make, it tastes a zillion times better than the supermarket version and its utility is endless, from tortilla chips and *sopes* to omelets and rice pilaf.

HERE'S WHAT YOU DO:

With a teaspoon or your fingers, remove the seeds from the tomato halves and shake out any accumulating juices. Cut each tomato half into julienne strips, then dice the strips. Place in a small bowl by themselves and allow to rest for 10 minutes to release any remaining juice and seeds.

Thinly slice, then mince the scallions. Transfer to a medium-size bowl and add the cilantro, jalapeño, and lime juice. Drain the tomatoes, then combine with the other ingredients. Stir everything together before adding the salt.

Stir again, taste, and adjust both the salt and lime as you see fit. The flavors should feel fresh in the mouth.

Eat the same day the salsa is prepared.

MAKE ABOUT 1½ CUPS SALSA

- 4 Roma tomatoes, sliced in half lengthwise
- 3 to 4 scallions, washed, roots and dark tops removed
- ¼ cup fresh cilantro leaves, washed, dried, and chopped finely
- ½ jalapeño chile pepper, seeded and minced
- Juice of ½ lime
- ½ teaspoon salt

STRAWBERRY AND PEPITA SALAD

V **GF**

I love throwing fruit into green salads and get particularly excited when in-season, lipstick red strawberries are part of the equation. The toasted pepitas (a.k.a. pumpkin seeds) lend a rich nuttiness, transforming a simple green salad into a fiesta.

HERE'S WHAT YOU DO:

Prepare the seasoning salt: In a small bowl, combine the salt, lime zest, and cayenne and stir until well blended.

Place the pepitas in a cast-iron skillet and toast over medium heat until they turn light golden brown, making sure they don't burn. They may snap, crackle, and pop as they heat up. Transfer to a small bowl, and while they're still hot, coat with ¼ teaspoon of the seasoning salt.

Place the strawberries in another bowl and add ¼ teaspoon of the seasoning salt, plus the brown sugar. Gently stir until the strawberries are evenly coated and seasoned.

Place the greens in a large salad bowl. Dust with ¼ teaspoon of the seasoning salt. In a small bowl, fork-whisk the lime juice and olive oil. Just before serving, dress the greens with the vinaigrette, turning with tongs or salad forks to evenly coat. Add the strawberries and pepitas and give everything one last toss before serving.

MAKES 6 SERVINGS

- ½ teaspoon salt
- ½ teaspoon lime zest (about 1 lime)
- ⅛ teaspoon ground cayenne
- ½ cup raw pepitas (hulled pumpkin seeds)
- 2 cups hulled and thinly sliced strawberries
- 1 teaspoon light or brown sugar
- 5 cups arugula or butter lettuce that has been washed, dried, and cut or torn into 2-inch pieces
- 1 tablespoon freshly squeezed lime juice
- 1 tablespoon olive oil

TOOLS: *Cast-iron skillet*

KITCHEN NOTES: *Pepitas are often found in the bulk areas of many supermarkets and natural foods markets, as well as Latin groceries.*

CHOCOLATE-CHILE PUDDING

GF **DO** **KIDDO**

- 4 ounces semi- or bittersweet chocolate, or ¾ cup semisweet chocolate chips
- 1 (12-ounce) package firm silken tofu, preferably organic
- ¾ cup granulated sugar
- 1 teaspoon vanilla extract
- 1 teaspoon ground cinnamon
- Generous pinch of ground cayenne
- ⅓ cup unsweetened milk of choice (coconut, cow's, soy)
- 1½ cups berries of choice

TOOLS: *Food processor or blender*

KITCHEN NOTES: *This will have more of a mousse-y texture and mouthfeel compared to the pumpkin pudding on page 58. I have used chocolate in both bar and chip form, and the results are equally delightful, so feel free to use what's on hand and available where you live. I've used everything from Ghirardelli chips to single-origin baking bars, and I'm always happy with the results.*

Even in the absence of milk solids, most baking chocolate is not guaranteed dairy-free, due to cross-contamination during processing. If dairy is an issue, be sure to read labels before buying.

Fifteen minutes. That's all you need to put this pudding together—without an instant-presto box of mix. Silken tofu is the magic ingredient here, fooling all traditional pudding lovers with its supercreamy mouthfeel.

HERE'S WHAT YOU DO:

Melt the chocolate: Pour a few inches of water into a small saucepan and place a metal bowl that fits snugly on top, yet without touching the water, to make a double boiler. Break the chocolate into smaller pieces (if using the bars) and place in the bowl. Over medium-low heat, allow the chocolate to completely melt, using a heatproof rubber spatula to stir and blend. Remove the bowl from the heat and let the chocolate cool for 5 minutes.

Plan B: Place the broken-up bar chocolate (or chocolate chips) in a microwaveable bowl and microwave for about 90 seconds, until melted. Stir to blend.

Place the tofu, with its liquid, in a food processor or blender. Add the sugar, vanilla, cinnamon, and cayenne, and blend until the tofu is creamy smooth and the sugar crystals are undetectable. Add the melted chocolate and blend, stopping to scrape the sides of the bowl, followed by the milk. Blend one last time; the mixture should be well integrated, creamy, and maybe even a little fluffy.

Transfer the pudding to a bowl, cover, and refrigerate for 1 hour. The pudding can be served immediately at room temperature, but is best when chilled. Serve in small bowls, topped with berries.

Leftovers will keep for a few days. The pudding may separate slightly, easily remedied by a few stirs.

MAKES SIX ⅓-CUP SERVINGS (WITH A LITTLE EXTRA FOR COOK'S TREAT)

SUMMER

when the great outdoors becomes one giant living room

SAVORING SUMMER SHINDIG

I'm an August baby, so summer is when I'm the happiest-go-luckiest kid in town, even on days when it's hot enough to fry an egg on the sidewalk. All year long, I wait in anticipation for that first night with the windows open and the gift of falling asleep to the greatest hits from the nocturnal insect world. I can hardly wait to wake with the sun and sit with my coffee, as the tomatoes flower and the bees stop by for breakfast. There is no other time in the year to eat your heart out in produce without getting bored. I make the case for okra and a savory pudding of corn kernels and lemongrass-infused coconut milk. I invite you to consider barbecue sauce with eggplant, a revelation on the tongue. Then come dance to the music, as Sly asked us to do back in 1968. Summer is so short it is but a dream.

ROASTED OR GRILLED OKRA **V** **GF**

There's no slicing, dicing, or worrying about mucilaginous slime; roasting (or grilling) okra pods whole dries, sweetens, and transforms them into umami-rich morsels. In fact, they remind me of roasted edamame—there's even a similar pull on the pod on that first bite—and they need little other than a smidge of oil and salt. In the height of summer, okra is tender and needs little cooking time; as the growing season wanes and the pods are woodier, they may need more time to soften.

HERE'S WHAT YOU DO:

Place the okra in a large bowl and add the oil and salt. With your hands, toss until the okra is completely coated with the seasonings. If using, coat with the paprika at this time.

To roast: Preheat the oven to 400°F and line a baking sheet with parchment paper. Place the okra in a single layer on the prepared pan and roast until fork tender, 10 to 15 minutes. (Check for doneness at the 10-minute mark.)

To grill: Heat the grill to 350°F and set it up for direct grilling. Have at the ready a cast-iron skillet. Grease grill grates and place a test okra on the grill to see if it is large enough not to fall through the grates. If the okra are large enough, place on the grill and cook until charred on two sides, 8 to 10 minutes. For smaller okra, place the skillet on the grill and grill-roast the okra in small batches until fork tender, 10 to 12 minutes.

Eat hot and sprinkle with more salt, as needed, and sesame seeds, if using.

MAKES 6 SERVINGS

- 1 pound okra, washed and dried
- 1 tablespoon olive oil, plus more for brushing
- ½ teaspoon salt, plus more to taste
- ½ teaspoon paprika (optional)
- ½ teaspoon sesame seeds (optional)

TOOLS: *Parchment paper (if roasting), cast-iron skillet (if grilling)*

CORN PUDDING V

Traditionally prepared when the sweet corn of summer is at its peak, corn pudding is iconic comfort food, and as such, is typically heavy on the dairy and eggs. In this version, I break with tradition and invite lemongrass-infused coconut milk and silken tofu to join the casserole party. The result is dreamy.

HERE'S WHAT YOU DO:

Remove the two outer layers of the lemongrass stalk and slice off the bulb end. Trim all but 4 inches of the stalk and slice the remaining piece in half, lengthwise.

Bring the coconut milk and water to a boil in a medium-size saucepan. Turn off the heat and add the two basil sprigs and the lemongrass.

Infuse for about 30 minutes, then drain and pour the infused coconut milk into the bowl of a blender or food processor. Add the silken tofu and puree, along with the sugar, curry powder, and salt.

Place the corn in a medium-size bowl and season with the lime juice, chile pepper, and scallions. Pour the pureed tofu over the corn, add the flour and cornmeal, and stir everything together. Season with the cayenne, stir, and taste for both heat and salt, reseasoning as needed.

Preheat the oven to 400°F. Lightly grease a 9-inch baking dish with the oil.

Pour the pudding into the prepared pan. Bake for 5 minutes, then lower the heat to 375°F. Bake for an additional 55 minutes, or until the center is just slightly jiggly and the top is golden. The edges should be some-what firm and slightly crusty.

Top the pudding with tomato halves and a chiffonade of basil.

Serve hot.

MAKES 6 SERVINGS

- 1 stalk lemongrass
- 1 (13-ounce) can coconut milk
- ½ cup water
- 2 leafy sprigs of basil, plus ¼ cup leaves, for garnish
- 1 (12-ounce) package firm silken tofu
- 1 teaspoon granulated sugar
- 1 teaspoon curry powder of your choice
- 1 teaspoon salt, plus more to taste
- 2 cups corn kernels (from about 4 medium-size ears of corn)
- Juice of ½ lime
- ½ fresh chile pepper of choice, seeded and minced
- ¼ cup scallions, roots and dark tops removed, sliced into thin rings
- 1 tablespoon all-purpose flour
- ¼ cup cornmeal
- Pinch of cayenne
- Neutral oil, for greasing the baking dish
- Garnish: ½ pint cherry or grape tomatoes, sliced in half

TOOLS: *Blender or food processor, 9-inch baking dish*

BARBECUED BAKED EGGPLANT
V **GF** **KIDDO**

ROASTED EGGPLANT STACKS:

- Olive oil or oil spray, for greasing
- 2 medium-size globe eggplants (about 1 pound each)
- Salt, for leaching
- ½ medium-size onion, root intact
- 1 to 1½ cups Finger-Licking Barbecue Sauce (page 147)
- 3 to 4 Roma tomatoes, cut into ½-inch slices

TOOLS: *13 by 9-inch baking dish, cast-iron skillet*

You can make the barbecue sauce in advance, as it will keep for about 5 days in the refrigerator. You won't use all of it, but you'll be glad to have leftovers.

HERE'S WHAT YOU DO:

Preheat the oven to 400°F. Grease two baking sheets with olive oil or cooking spray, as well as a 13 by 9-inch baking dish.

Slice the eggplant into ½-inch rounds. Place the eggplant on a rack in a single layer and sprinkle salt on top to help release the water content. Allow to leach for about 15 minutes.

Meanwhile, place a cast-iron skillet over medium heat and set the onion cut side down in the pan. Allow to char for about 5 minutes, then transfer to the oven to roast for an additional 15 minutes. The onion should be charred and softened; if not, cook for an additional 10 minutes. Set aside until cool enough to handle. (Prefer to grill? Place the onion, cut side down, in the skillet on a hot grill and roast until charred and softened, 10 to 15 minutes.)

With a paper towel, pat the eggplant dry before cooking, whether roasting or grilling.

Place the eggplant rounds in a single layer on both baking sheets. Roast for 15 minutes. Turn and roast on the second side for an additional 10 minutes, for a total of 25 minutes.

(Grilled option: With a brush, grease the grate. Grill using the direct method, making sure the eggplant does not burn. Cook for 7 to 10 minutes on the first side, turn, and grill on the second side for an additional 7 minutes.)

Lower the oven temperature to 350°F.

Cut the onion into thin half-moons; it will be soft and the pieces may be imperfect, but that's okay.

Place 3 tablespoons of the barbecue sauce in the prepared dish, and spread until the surface is covered.

Assemble the eggplant stacks: Arrange twelve eggplant rounds in a single layer in the sauce-lined dish. Apply 1 teaspoon of the barbecue sauce to each eggplant round, followed by a tomato slice, then two onion pieces. Repeat with another cycle of twelve more eggplant rounds, 1 teaspoon of the sauce, one tomato slice, and two onion pieces. The stacks should be crowned with a third eggplant round.

Cover the entire dish with barbecue sauce; you'll probably use ¼ to ½ cup. Cover with foil and bake until the sauce is bubbly and the stacks are fork tender, about 40 minutes.

You may make in advance and reheat when ready to serve. This is equally good hot or at room temperature.

MAKES 6 SERVINGS

PLUM FILLING:

- 1½ cups plums (3 to 5 plums; amount will vary depending on variety and size)
- 1½ tablespoons cornstarch or quick-cooking tapioca
- Pinch of salt
- 1 teaspoon vanilla extract
- 3 to 4 tablespoons granulated sugar, to taste
- Slight squeeze of ½ lemon
- 2 tablespoons apricot jam

PLUM GALETTE

At the height of summer, sun-kissed plums need little adornment and really get to strut their stuff in this freeform tart. As with the blood orange galette in the New Year's chapter (page 88), we're playing with the butter–olive oil pie dough I've been talking about throughout these pages. If you've never made a galette, it's more rustic both in presentation and sometimes texture. I often like to describe it as a big Pop-Tart.

If plums are not your thing or out of reach, try playing with its stone fruit cousin, the apricot. Do steer clear of peaches, which are too juicy for an open-face tart.

HERE'S WHAT YOU DO:

Plum Filling

Cut the plums in half around the pit, then cut into thin slices about ⅛-inch thick. Place the plums in a medium-size bowl and add the cornstarch, salt, vanilla, and 3 tablespoons of the sugar. Stir gently until the fruit is completely coated. Taste and add more sugar as needed, then add the small bit of lemon juice. Let the fruit sit in its juices for about 20 minutes.

Enlightened Pie Dough

Place the olive oil in a small bowl and set aside.

Place the water in a small saucepan and heat until very hot. It need not be boiling but should be pretty close.

While the water is heating, measure out the flour. Remove 1 tablespoon and reserve for rolling out the dough. (You may need a little bit more that your reserve for second rolling.) Place in the food processor, along with the salt and the baking powder, and pulse a few times just to mix.

Add the butter. Pulse until the mixture looks and feels like fluffy sand. You should not be able to see butter clumps.

Measure out ¼ cup (4 tablespoons) of the water and add to the oil. With a fork, whisk together; it will look like a vinaigrette.

Pour the oil mixture on top of the flour mixture, and pulse until the dough just comes together. It may slightly pull away from the sides of the bowl. The dough should feel soft, warm, and pliable, not hard and crumbly. If the dough looks as if it needs more liquid, add the hot water in 1-tablespoon increments, pulse, and check the softness of the dough.

Lightly dust your rolling surface with some of the reserved flour, and place the dough on top. Surround the dough with both hands to let it know you're there, or as my pie co-conspirator Kate McDermott says, "give it a good handshake," molding it into a cohesive lump.

Roll the dough in quick, even strokes, making a quarter-turn after every few strokes. As you rotate and roll the dough, check regularly to make sure the dough is not sticking. (A dough scraper is helpful at this stage). The immediate goal is to make a rectangle roughly 9 by 11-inches. (Don't worry if it's not exact.)

Fold the dough like a letter: Starting from a short edge, fold over a third of your dough. Take the opposite edge and fold it to the middle, covering the first fold.

Make a quarter-turn, then roll out the dough into a new rectangle, dusting with flour as needed. Make another letter fold with the dough.

Give the dough another quarter-turn, and roll the dough in all four directions—north, south, east, west. Fold the dough in half into a 4- to 5-inch square packet. Roll lightly on top to seal the layers and surround the edges with both hands to tidy the dough.

Wrap the dough in plastic and allow to rest in the refrigerator for a brief 10 minutes. Unlike an all-butter dough, this dough never goes into a deep sleep and gets cold; think of it as a brief catnap after all that rolling and folding.

Preheat the oven to 425°F.

In a microwave oven or in a small saucepan, heat up the jam until melty, like a sauce.

Roll out the dough on the rolling surface. Dust both the top and bottom of the dough with extra flour, as needed. With more of those deft, even strokes, roll the dough into a 9- or 10-inch circle or rectangle.

Brush the surface of the dough with a thin layer of the melted jam, leaving a 2-inch border all around.

▶ ▶ ▶

ENLIGHTENED PIE DOUGH:

- 4 tablespoons olive oil
- ½ cup water
- 2 cups all-purpose flour, plus more for dusting
- ¼ teaspoon salt
- ¼ teaspoon baking powder
- 4 tablespoons butter, cut into tablespoon-size pieces
- 2 to 3 tablespoons apricot jam
- Egg white wash: 1 egg white, beaten with 1 tablespoon water
- 1 to 2 tablespoons granulated or coarse sugar

TOOLS: *Food processor, dough scraper, silicone baking mat or parchment paper, silicone or pastry brush*

Strain the fruit before placing on top of the dough. Arrange the fruit in concentric circles, in overlapping fashion, again within the 2-inch border.

With the help of a dough scraper (or the surface underneath), lift the margins of the dough, section by section, over the filling, pressing dough edges when they meet. As much as one-third of the filling in the center will be exposed; that's okay.

Brush the top of the dough with the egg white wash, then sprinkle lightly with the sugar.

Transfer the galette (and its liner underneath) to a baking sheet and into the refrigerator for a quick 5-minute chill. While the galette is chilling, heat the jam in the microwave until melty and saucelike, about 30 seconds. Brush the exposed fruit with the jam, which will make them glisten.

Place the galette in the preheated oven and bake for 5 minutes. Lower the heat to 375°F and bake for an additional 35 to 40 minutes, checking at minute 30 for doneness. The galette is done when the crust is golden and the fruit is bubbling.

Grab the two ends of the parchment or baking mat and transfer the galette to a rack, allowing it to cool for about 1 hour.

MAKES 6 TO 8 SERVINGS

MOVEABLE FEAST/ DINING AL FRESCO

I'm a fool for eating al fresco, even right outside the back door. For this Leo baby ruled by the sun, a meal taken out of doors—even a few feet away from the kitchen—is always more delicious (or at least it seems that way). But what really sends me over the moon is packing up a bag or a basket of goodies and toting them off-site—to the river's edge, the seashore, the park down the street—for the ultimate moveable feast. Ants and mosquitoes be damned; summer is a short-lived opportunity to take off our coat, stay a while, and eat with our hands. It's a chance to break bread in the absence of walls and furniture, when we make a table out of our lap and we're served by elves that magically appear out of the picnic basket. For a midsummer night's spell, we're somewhere else and the living is easy.

All of the following dishes can easily be packed for travel in a basket or cooler. (A few dry ice packs are always helpful to keep things cold.) For the sandwiches, I recommend a layer of parchment before foil, and for everything else, plastic containers to minimize leakage. Bring a handful of cloth napkins and enjoy the adventure!

KID-FRIENDLY MENU IDEAS

My four-year-old pint-size pal Ethan and I have been spending time in the kitchen since he was about six months old. I remember watching him lick his lips after his first spoonful of lentils. He's a good eater and continues to try new things, but especially when he's standing by my side at the counter. While testing the recipes for Sandra's Sopes and Sofrito-Seasoned Black Beans, Ethan insisted on his own batch of masa harina, which he rolled into balls and flattened with a tortilla press. Far from perfect, Ethan's *sopes* were a labor of love, and he could not wait to try the results of his handiwork.

All of the recipes in this chapter received high marks from testers with kids, who licked their plates and asked for more. It's an exciting day when this country's future sees a world beyond chicken nuggets and asks for more of those yummy vegetables, please.

KOD'S GRANOLA `KIDDO`

The kids will love this stuff, but so will you. Making your own gra-nola is so cinchy and straightforward that you may never buy the store-bought version again. Use the ingredients as a guide but feel free to tinker with the mix of fruit, nuts, and seeds and put your own spin on things. With an all-purpose mojo, homespun granola will wow them at slumber party breakfasts, after the game, or on those long road trips. If you've got a reluctant kitchen helper in your midst, this is a great ice breaker.

HERE'S WHAT YOU DO:

In a large mixing bowl, combine the oats, buckwheat groats, cinnamon, dried fruit, nuts, and seeds. Stir to mix.

Preheat the oven to 300°F. Line a roasting pan or a few baking trays with parchment paper.

Pour the honey, maple syrup, and oil into a small saucepan and warm over low heat until the mixture thins, about 2 minutes. Stir to keep from burning. Do not boil the mixture.

Pour the warm mixture on top of the dry ingredients, stirring with a rubber spatula or wooden spoon until well coated.

Spread the granola on the prepared pan or trays until evenly distributed.

Bake for a total of 45 minutes, stirring every 15 minutes to prevent burning and sticking. The granola is done when it's glistening and golden.

Allow to cool completely; the granola will crisp up within 30 minutes. Store in an airtight container.

MAKES ABOUT 10 CUPS, OR 20 HALF-CUP SERVINGS

- 4 cups old-fashioned rolled oats (do not use instant)
- ¼ cup untoasted buckwheat groats (a.k.a. kasha)
- ¼ teaspoon ground cinnamon
- 1½ cups dried fruit: any combination of raisins, cherries, cranberries, or blueberries
- 2 cups unsalted nuts: Any combination of walnuts, almonds, pecans, pistachios, or cashews, chopped roughly or left whole
- 1 cup raw sunflower seeds
- ¼ cup sesame seeds
- ½ cup of your favorite flavor of honey, preferably local
- ¾ cup good-quality pure maple syrup
- ¼ cup neutral oil

TOOLS: *Parchment paper*

FOURTH OF JULY

The Fourth of July has always held a sweet place in my heart; it was the day when I woke up early, walked to the corner, and watched the neighborhood parade, a marching assortment of town characters that always included some old dude driving an antique convertible. Even during my college years, I loved to take in the parade. Within a few short hours, the air would fill with the smoke of charcoal briquets, shortly followed by the unforgettable smells of grilled bones and gristle. There would be music and paper plates and eating under a tree. It never got old. (It still doesn't.) The menu that follows is really the work of small farmers who harvest the cherries for my pie, the romaine for the ever-surprising and superfast wok salad, the blueberries for my two-bean salad (yes, blueberries and beans!), and the garlic scapes for my pesto, a limited-edition item that must be experienced. They are truly patriots, looking after the land.

GARLIC SCAPE PESTO–STUFFED CHERRY TOMATOES `DO` `GF`

I talk a lot about eating seasonally, but this dish is more like eating in the moment. You see, the scape is a part of the garlic plant at a particular time in its growth. Like other members of the Allium family (leeks, onions, shallots), garlic grows underground into a soft, onion-like bulb. As the bulb gets harder (and more like the garlic we know), it produces a green shoot that pokes its way through the ground. It's pliable enough to curl into tendrils, and in addition to being beautiful, it's mighty fine eating. Farmers clip scapes so that the underground bulbs can keep growing, and bring them to farmers' markets in June or early July, depending on where you live. Make some of this pesto and live in the moment!

HERE'S WHAT YOU DO:

Place the scapes and walnuts in the bowl of a food processor and whiz until well combined and somewhat smooth. Slowly drizzle in the oil and process until integrated. With a rubber spatula, scoop the pesto into a small bowl. Add the Parmigiano-Reggiano (if using), then add the salt and pepper to taste. You'll end up with a total of ¾ cup of pesto.

Prepare the tomatoes: Slice off the tops with a small serrated knife. With a ⅛-teaspoon measure, gently scoop out the seeds and juice. Place the tomatoes, cut side down, on a rack to drain, about 15 minutes, with a paper towel underneath to catch any juice.

Slice off the bottoms of the tomatoes to create a flat edge so they can sit upright. With the ⅛-teaspoon measure, fill the tomatoes with the pesto, using a chopstick to poke it inside.

Serve on a platter, with toothpicks. May be assembled a few hours before serving; cover with plastic and keep in the refrigerator.

Store the rest of the pesto in an airtight container in the refrigerator, where it will keep for a week. Try it as a sandwich spread, mixed into pasta, or atop boiled potatoes.

MAKES 6 SERVINGS

- 1 cup garlic scapes (8 or 9 scapes), top flowery part removed, cut into ¼-inch slices
- ⅓ cup unsalted walnuts, chopped roughly
- ¾ cup olive oil
- ¼ to ½ cup grated Parmigiano-Reggiano cheese (optional)
- ½ teaspoon salt
- Freshly ground black pepper
- 1 pint cherry tomatoes, washed

TOOLS: *Food processor*

KITCHEN NOTES: *Admittedly, stuffing itty-bitty cherry tomatoes does require some channeling of one's inner Martha, so be advised. Nothing is difficult about this dish, but it does require some patience and a steady hand to scoop out the tomatoes and fill them. The good news: They are quite the eye candy and will wow all the guests.*

TWO-BEAN AND BLUEBERRY SALAD V GF

There's great color contrast going on in this salad, but the real surprise is how well the sweet blueberries play with the legumes, as well as the corn kernels (and the bell pepper). . . .

- 1 cup dried black beans
- 1 cup dried white beans (cannellini or great northern)
- 2 cloves garlic, peeled and left whole
- 2 teaspoons salt, plus more to taste
- 2 tablespoons olive oil, plus more to taste
- 1 to 2 limes
- ½ to 1 teaspoon chili powder blend
- ½ to 1 teaspoon ground coriander
- Freshly ground black pepper
- ½ to ¾ cup fresh or frozen corn kernels* (1 to 2 medium-size ears of corn, if fresh)
- 1 cup blueberries
- 1 cup seeded and diced red, orange, or yellow bell pepper (from 1 medium-size pepper)
- ¼ to ½ cup scallions, roots and dark tops removed, sliced into thin rings
- ¼ to ½ cup of any combination of finely chopped fresh leafy herbs: cilantro, parsley, mint, or basil

HERE'S WHAT YOU DO:

Place the beans in separate bowls and cover each with about 3 inches of water. Soak for at least 4 hours. (In warmer climes, soak the beans in the refrigerator to avoid sprouting or fermentation.)

Drain the beans from their respective bowls. Transfer to two separate pots fitted with lids and cover with about 7 cups of water; you're looking for a few inches of water above the beans. Add 1 clove of garlic to each pot of beans, and bring each to a boil. Cook at a hard boil for 5 minutes. Cover, lower the heat, and cook at a gentle simmer.

At minute 20 of simmering, stir in 1 teaspoon of the salt to each pot. At minute 45, check the beans for doneness. Cook in 10-minute increments until the beans arrive at the al dente stage, keeping in mind that cooking times may vary, depending on the age of the beans.

Remove the garlic cloves, drain the beans of their respective cooking liquids and transfer to separate bowls. Add 1 tablespoon of the olive oil and the juice of ½ lime to each bowl, gently stirring to coat and season the beans. Taste from each bowl and make sure you are tasting lime.

Add the chili powder blend to the black beans, and the ground coriander to the white beans. Start with the minimum amount suggested and taste after mixing, adding more as needed. Season each bowl of beans with salt and pepper to taste.

Note: If making in advance, this is a good stopping point. Refrigerate the beans (which you may now combine) until ready to mix in the rest of the ingredients and serve.

Transfer all of the beans to a large mixing bowl.

Prep the corn: If using frozen kernels, cook briefly in a small saucepan, along with 1 cup of boiling water, for 3 minutes. You can also thaw the

▶ ▶ ▶

KITCHEN NOTES: *I'm insisting on dried beans here because texture is fundamental to the success of this salad. Canned beans are just too soft, and with all the subsequent stirring of seasonings, they get even softer (read: mushy). Mushy is what happened to me, too, when I cooked dried beans until tender to the bite as I do for a pot of chili. Again, with all the stirring and tossing, the beans lose some of their structural integrity. Slightly undercooking the beans (think: al dente) yields the best results.*

Because the beans need both soaking and cooking time, these steps can be done in advance and the chopping and seasoning of the salad can be done in about 30 minutes before serving.

*On using fresh corn: I recommend that you give your corn a quick stint in boiling water. Remove the husk and silk from each ear and slice off the kernels with a sharp knife. Place the kernels in 1 cup of boiling water and cook for 60 seconds. Scoop out the kernels with a slotted spoon or spider sieve and rinse under cold water.

corn in the microwave with ¼ cup of water, for 2 minutes. Drain and place on top of the beans.

Place the blueberries, bell pepper, and scallions directly on top of the beans. Toss everything together (this minimizes the mush factor explained earlier), and taste.

Just before serving, add the herbs of your choice.

MAKES 8 TO 10 SERVINGS

GRILLED ZUCCHINI HERO `DO`

Where I grew up, we didn't use the word *hero* for a big honkin' sandwich on a long roll; we called it a hoagie. In this case, hero seems appropriate because in a grill zone of burgers, franks, and ribs (or the frozen veggie patties out of a box), this sandwich, savory and scrumptious, has the goods to save the day. I do believe I've found a new lover.

The flavors—a symphony of everything there is to love about summer produce—will transport you to Provence or somewhere equally marvelously Mediterranean. There's the sweetness of roasted red peppers, the char of zucchini "planks" marinated in a balsamic vinaigrette, and peppery arugula, all book-ended by a schmear of goat cheese and fennel seed–studded olive tapenade. Better still, the fixin's work beautifully as a salad. The details for the variation follow.

HERE'S WHAT YOU DO:

Hero

Make the marinade: Place the olive oil, vinegar, salt, and oregano in a small bowl and fork-whisk until well blended.

With a sharp knife, remove both ends of the zucchini. Your end goal is zucchini "planks" about 4 inches long. For 8- to 12-inch zucchini, cut the lengths in half (or thirds). For larger zucchini, cut into fourths.

Stand a zucchini half on one end so it's upright. From top to bottom, cut into "planks" about ¼-inch thick. You should end up with eight to ten pieces per zucchini.

Transfer the prepped zucchini into a dish and pour the marinade on top, turning until it's evenly coated. Marinate for about 30 minutes.

(Outdoor option: Place the zucchini and marinade in a zip-style plastic bag and keep in a cooler until ready to grill.)

▶ ▶ ▶

- 2 tablespoons olive oil, plus more for brushing grill
- 2 tablespoons balsamic vinegar
- ½ teaspoon salt, plus more to taste
- 1 teaspoon dried oregano
- 4 medium-size zucchini
- 1 teaspoon fennel seeds
- 1 cup kalamata olives, pitted
- ¼ to ½ teaspoon red chile pepper flakes, to taste
- Zest of 1 lemon
- 6 (4-inch) soft round buns or 6-inch hero-style rolls, toasted lightly
- 3 ounces plain soft goat cheese
- 2 medium-size or large red bell peppers, roasted,* seeded, and sliced thinly
- 1 bunch arugula or spinach, washed, stemmed, and dried

TOOLS: *Cast-iron skillet, food processor or mortar and pestle*

While the zucchini marinates, make the olive spread: Place the fennel seeds in a cast-iron skillet and toast over medium heat, about 90 seconds. The seeds will turn slightly golden. Transfer to a small bowl.

Pulverize the olives in a food processor or mash in a mortar and pestle. The olives should be pasty with a little bit of texture. Add the olives to the same bowl with the fennel seeds, along with the lemon zest. Stir everything together until well blended.

Prepare a grill for direct cooking and generously brush the grates with olive oil. (Indoor option: Use the ridged side of a grill pan over medium-high heat.)

Place the zucchini on the hot grates and allow to sear on the first side, 2 to 3 minutes. Turn and cook on the second side for an additional 2 to 3 minutes.

Assemble the sandwiches: Spread 2 teaspoons of the olive spread on one bun half, and 1 teaspoon of the goat cheese on the other half.

Place four zucchini planks on top of the olive spread, followed by ⅛ cup of the roasted peppers.

Tear or cut the arugula in half, and place ¼ to ½ cup on top of the goat cheese layer. Book-end the sandwich and cut in half.

Salad Variation

Place the greens in a large salad bowl. Squeeze the lemon half all over the greens, then sprinkle with the salt. Place ½ cup of the roasted peppers on top of the greens, adding more as you see fit. Drop the olive spread by the teaspoon all over the greens, followed by the goat cheese in the same manner. Lay the zucchini on top in a circle.

MAKES 6 SERVINGS

SALAD VARIATION (GF):

- 5 cups arugula or spinach, washed, dried, and stemmed
- A few squeezes of ½ lemon
- A sprinkling of Maldon flakes or another coarse salt, to taste
- ½ to 1 cup thinly sliced roasted peppers
- 5 tablespoons olive spread
- ⅛ cup goat cheese
- 20 to 24 zucchini planks

KITCHEN NOTES: *Originally I noted that the average length of a zucchini is 8 inches, but that's being unrealistic. After all, at the peak of their season, the prolific zucchini can grow into an enormous creature with the length and girth of a 6-foot-long hoagie. Okay, so maybe I'm exaggerating, but we've all grown or been gifted with zukes of extraordinary proportions. All of this is to say, as long as your zucchini is cut to 4 inches long, you're in business. Both the roasted peppers and the olive spread can be made in advance to make the day of assembly a snap.*

How to Roast a Bell Pepper: Preheat the oven to 400°F. Line a baking sheet with parchment paper. Slice off the stem end and shake out the seeds. Place the pepper on the prepared baking sheet and roast until the skin is charred all over and the pepper has collapsed, about 40 minutes. Transfer the pepper to a sealed container or paper bag so that it can sweat and loosen its skin. Once cool (about 15 minutes), remove the skin with your hands or a paring knife. Do not rinse, as this dilutes the roasted flavor. Keeps well in an airtight container in the refrigerator for about 1 week.

- 3 tablespoons neutral oil
- 2 cloves whole garlic, peeled and smashed
- 1½ teaspoons peeled and minced fresh ginger
- 1½ bunches romaine lettuce, washed thoroughly, dried, and cut into 2-inch pieces (7 to 9 cups)
- Generous pinch of granulated sugar
- 15 to 18 cherry tomatoes (or another small variety), halved
- 1 tablespoon soy sauce or wheat-free tamari

TOOLS: *14-inch wok (preferably carbon-steel, not nonstick!) or a 12-inch, heavy-bottomed stainless-steel skillet*

KITCHEN NOTES: *Lettuce must be as dry as possible or else it will yield a stew-like, soggy result. You're looking for a light sear.*

WOK SALAD ⒱

It may seem counterintuitive to stand over a hot wok at the height of summer, but frankly it's one of the easiest, quickest ways to cook at this time of the year. With inspiration and guidance over the years from cookbook author and wok laureate Grace Young, I've put a stir-fry spin on a simple summer salad that comes together lickety-split. Warning: This is so tasty you may not want to share.

HERE'S WHAT YOU DO:

Heat the wok over high heat until, as Grace says, "a bead of water vaporizes within 1 to 2 seconds of contact."

Swirl in the oil so that it's equally distributed and add the garlic and ginger. With a Chinese metal spatula or metal pancake spatula, stir-fry—quickly and continuously scoop and toss—until fragrant, about 20 seconds. Add the lettuce, sprinkle the sugar on top, and stir-fry until it is wilted and bright green, 2 to 3 minutes. Add the tomatoes and soy sauce and continue to stir-fry, tossing vigorously, until the tomatoes are warm and slightly softened, about 30 seconds.

Eat hot.

MAKES 6 SALAD-SIZE SERVINGS

CHERRY PIE WITH ENLIGHTENED PIE DOUGH

CHERRY FILLING:

- 4 to 6 cups sweet or sour cherries, pitted
- 1 tablespoon quick-cooking or instant tapioca
- 2 tablespoons all-purpose flour
- Pinch of salt
- 1 slight squeeze of ½ lemon
- 1 cup granulated sugar, plus more to taste
- 1 teaspoon almond extract

TOOLS: *9-inch pie pan*

As detailed in the Thanksgiving chapter (page 43), this is a different kind of pie dough that breaks with tradition. As part of my effort to lighten up dessert, I worked with pie expert Kate McDermott to develop a fifty-fifty butter–olive oil dough. Our recipe is an unorthodox combination of techniques that includes the hot water method traditionally used for meat pies in England and a "letter" fold that encourages the flaky layers reminiscent of a butter crust. This dough cooperates best when about body temperature, a stark departure from the traditional all-butter crust, which is typically very cold.

HERE'S WHAT YOU DO:

Cherry Filling

Place the cherries in the pie pan until they are about ½ inch below the rim. Save the rest for another use. Wipe clean the pie pan and transfer the cherries to a large bowl.

Add the remaining ingredients and gently stir until the fruit is evenly coated. Taste for sugar and add more as needed (you still will be able to tell while the fruit is frozen). Drain of liquid before filling the dough-lined pan.

Enlightened Pie Dough

Place the olive oil in a small bowl.

Place the water in a small saucepan and heat until very hot. It need not be boiling but should be pretty close.

While the water is heating, measure out the flour. Remove 1½ tablespoons and reserve for rolling out the dough. (You may need more than your reserve, for rolling.) Place in a food processor, along with the salt and the baking powder. Pulse a few times just to mix.

Add the butter. Pulse until the mixture looks and feels like fluffy sand. You should not be able to see butter clumps.

▶ ▶ ▶

ENLIGHTENED PIE DOUGH:

- 6 tablespoons olive oil
- ½ cup water
- 3 cups all-purpose flour, plus more for dusting
- ¼ teaspoon plus ⅛ teaspoon salt
- ¼ teaspoon plus ⅛ teaspoon baking powder
- 6 tablespoons cold butter, cut into tablespoon-size pieces
- 1 egg white, beaten with 1 tablespoon of water
- Granulated sugar, for sprinkling

TOOLS: *Food processor, rolling pin, 5-inch dough scraper, silicone baking mat or parchment paper, ruler or measuring tape*

Measure out 6 tablespoons of the hot water and add to the oil. With a fork, whisk together; it will look like a vinaigrette.

Pour the oil mixture on top of the flour mixture and pulse until the dough just comes together. It may slightly pull away from the sides of the bowl. The dough should be warm and feel soft and pliable, not hard and crumbly. If the dough looks and feels as if it needs more liquid, add the hot water in 1-tablespoon increments, pulse, and check the softness of the dough.

Lightly dust your rolling surface with some of the reserved flour and place the dough on top. Surround the dough with both hands to let it know you're there, or as Kate says, "give it a good handshake," molding it into a thick, cohesive lump.

Roll the dough in quick, even strokes, making a quarter-turn after every few strokes. As you rotate and roll the dough, check regularly to make sure the dough is not sticking. (A dough scraper is helpful at this stage.) The immediate goal is to make a rectangle roughly 9 by 11-inches. (Don't worry if it's not exact.)

Fold the dough like a letter: Starting from a short edge, fold over a third of your dough. Take the opposite edge and fold it to the middle, covering the first fold.

Make a quarter-turn, then roll out the dough into a new rectangle, dusting with flour as needed.

Make another letter fold with the dough. Give the dough another quarter-turn and roll the dough in all four directions—north, south, east, west. Fold the dough in half into a 4- to 5-inch square packet. Roll lightly on the top to seal the layers and surround the edges with both hands to tidy the dough.

Cut the dough into two halves, wrap each in plastic and allow to rest in the refrigerator for 10 minutes. Unlike an all-butter dough, this dough never goes into a deep sleep and gets cold; think of it as a brief catnap after all that rolling and folding.

Meanwhile, preheat the oven to 425°F.

Lightly dust the rolling surface and roll out one dough half. With more of those quick, even strokes, roll the dough into a circle until it's about 1 inch larger than your pie pan. Fold the dough in half and transfer to the pie pan. (A dough scraper can help with the lifting.)

Press the dough into the pan, making sure that it's completely covered. Strain the fruit if necessary and fill the lined pan.

Roll out the remaining dough half in the same manner, and fold in half to transfer and lay on top of the filling. Carefully unfold the dough to cover the entire filling. Make sure that the edges of the top and bottom dough layers meet before you trim any overhanging dough with kitchen shears or a paring knife. Use any extra dough to patch holes or tears.

Seal the top by pressing the edges of the dough with the prongs of a fork. Make sure that the edges are well sealed, to minimize filling seepage.

Make a few slashes on the top of the dough with a paring knife. (I like to make four or five in a circular pattern in the center; feel free to get creative.) Brush with the egg white wash, then lightly sprinkle with the sugar.

Transfer the pie to the refrigerator for a quick 5-minute chill.

Place on a baking sheet and bake for 5 minutes. Lower the heat to 400°F and bake for an additional 50 to 55 minutes. The crust will be golden and the filling will bubble.

Remove the pie from the baking sheet and let cool on a rack for about 90 minutes so that the filling can set.

MAKES A DOUBLE-CRUST 9-INCH PIE

KITCHEN NOTES: *Make the filling first so that it's ready to go as soon as the dough is rolled out. As for the dough, have all of the ingredients at the ready and measured before you get started.*

I recommend using a silicone baking mat or parchment paper as the rolling surface. Either one is temperature neutral and helps to keep your beautiful dough from sticking. If all you have in the house is plastic wrap, use that. If you've got a love affair with your marble counter top, go for it.

Cherries greatly vary in size which explains the wide range in amounts suggested. If using frozen cherries, do not thaw; make the filling while the fruit is still frozen. For a thickener, Kate recommends, in addition to the flour, quick-cooking tapioca, which "snugs up" those cherries.

VANILLA-HONEY FROZEN YOGURT

GF **KIDDO**

- 1 quart 2% or full-fat "traditional" plain Greek yogurt
- 4 teaspoons vanilla extract
- ¾ to 1 cup honey, to taste

TOOLS: *Electric ice-cream maker*

KITCHEN NOTES: *Greek yogurt is the new darling of the yogurt world. Essentially, it's plain yogurt that's been strained of its liquid whey, giving it a creamier texture and fuller mouthfeel, which is key to a sumptuous frozen dessert. If it has yet to arrive in your local supermarket, you can strain full-fat plain yogurt through cheesecloth for about 30 minutes and get the same effects. Depending on the brand, Greek yogurt is available in non-fat, 2%, or "traditional," another way of saying full-fat. For this dessert, leave the nonfat variety on the shelf.*

A note on honey: The closer it comes from neighborhood beehives, the tastier and more gratifying, in my opinion. Eating the nectar from local flowers is a simple way to better understand the natural environment around you and appreciate the hard work of those busy bees. I've given a range on honey amounts, depending on your sweet tooth.

Unlike my husband and nearly everyone I know, I will not be requesting ice cream as part of my last supper. While I certainly appreciate small-batch, artisanal ice cream and gelato, I rarely can stomach more than a few spoonfuls. The stuff is just too rich for me. It makes sense; a cup of heavy cream contains 88 grams of total fat. But give me a cup of frozen yogurt, particularly of the home-churned variety, and I'm all smiles. Compared to ice cream, making fro-yo is a blink of an eye. Without eggs to cook or cream to scald, home-style frozen yogurt is essentially plain Greek yogurt (just 20 to 22 grams of total fat per cup, depending on brand), sweetened and flavored to your fancy, then chilled before a short stint in an electric ice-cream maker. For those balking at the idea of buying a new appliance, may I suggest splitting the cost with a friend or neighbor and making your first batch of fro-yo together. I predict the creamiest of custody battles.

HERE'S WHAT YOU DO:

Place all the ingredients in a medium-size bowl and stir well. Taste for sweetness and add more as needed. Cover and refrigerate for at least 1 hour.

Pour the mixture into an ice-cream maker and freeze, according to the manufacturer's instructions, about 30 minutes. The mixture will be extremely creamy, kind of like soft-serve ice cream.

Transfer the frozen yogurt into an airtight container and place in the freezer for 1 to 2 hours.

MAKES 1 QUART FROZEN YOGURT

FRO-YO AFFOGATO

This classic coffee drink is typically made with gelato, which is Italian for ice cream. I test the lower-fat waters with frozen yogurt, which works like a champ.

HERE'S WHAT YOU DO:

Place the frozen yogurt into a 2-ounce cup (single) or 4-ounce cup (double). Pour your desired amount of hot espresso over the yogurt. Serve immediately with a spoon.

PER SERVING:

- 1 to 2 scoops Vanilla-Honey Frozen Yogurt (page 202)
- 1½ ounces brewed espresso* (for a single); 2 to 3 ounces (for a double)

Using a stovetop pot or single-cup electric machine, brew the espresso according to the manufacturer's instructions.

PUTTING UP SEASONAL PRODUCE: KOD'S PRESERVED PANTRY

I came to home canning much in the way I did to yoga, curious yet reserved. Once I took those first steps onto the mat in 2002, I knew yoga would be more than a hobby I dabbled in; it would become an integral part of my life.

And so it goes with canning: Once I learned the practical how-tos, I discovered just how vital canning is to my well-being. As my canning mentor and dear friend Jeanne Sauvage says, canning is "preserving summer in a jar." It instills an appreciation of produce at its tastiest, ripest moments and gives us a second chance to relive those moments when the season is long gone. It teaches us to connect to the continuous flow of the seasons wherever we live, and perhaps to the people who grow fresh food and bring it to market. Because it's a time-consuming project that requires collaboration, it fosters trust and intimacy among friends that is unlike any I've ever known. What was at first a bunch of acquaintances made on Twitter, I founded Canning Across America in 2009, an ad hoc collective of food-loving folk united in its mission to revive the lost art of putting up food.

Every year, I expand my pantry of preserved goods, which now includes marinara sauce, dilly beans, and hot sauce. The small handful of recipes that follow will allow you to see if canning is for you; if nothing else, you'll have a grand old time catching up with a friend.

A FEW PRACTICAL NOTES BEFORE YOU GET STARTED

I use the water bath method for all of these canning recipes. This is one of the home canning methods approved by the USDA and what I recommend for new canners. There's no need for fancy gizmos, but there is a definitive list of tools that make the process easier and safer.

REQUIRED

CANNING JARS: I use the two-part lids (metal ring and flat lid with rubber gasket) sold by Ball and Kerr brands to seal my jars. They come in a variety of sizes and are sold in hardware stores and supermarkets. The jars and the rings are reusable for future canning seasons, but the lids must be replaced.

CANNING RACK: This keeps the jars from rattling around in rapidly boiling water. Available in metal and heatproof plastic (yes, it works!) on the same shelves as the jars.

DEEP POT FITTED WITH A LID: You may already have something in the cabinets—deep and wide enough for the canning rack, and tall enough that at least 1 inch of water covers the jars. Before buying one, ask a friend for a short-term loan.

JAR LIFTER: Also known as canning tongs. You can use rubberized cooking tongs in a pinch, but a wide-gripped jar lifter offers more stability as you move jars in and out of hot water (the Secure-Lift Jar Lifter by Ball works like a champ).

KITCHEN TOWELS: Maybe it seems obvious, but you want about four clean, dry towels on hand for wiping the jar rims clean before fitting with lids, and on which to place the cooling jars from the water bath.

HIGHLY RECOMMENDED

WIDE-MOUTHED FUNNEL: This sits snugly in the mouth of a canning jar and helps you to fill jars efficiently and with less mess. Sold with canning supplies.

RECOMMENDED BUT NOT A DEAL BREAKER

CANDY THERMOMETER: This is particularly helpful when cooking fruit to a gelled state for jam or marmalade. Sold in cookware stores and sometimes hardware stores.

LADLE: I've filled jars with ladles and without, and the ladle always makes me feel more in control.

NONMETAL CHOPSTICK: By running a nonmetal flat-edged item along the inside edge of your filled jars, you're helping remove any air bubbles that may otherwise get trapped, potentially impeding an effective seal. Companies such as Ball sell them as "bubble removers." Honestly, I sometimes forget this step and still get a seal, but it's a step worth doing.

ADDITIONAL TIDBITS

Canning is not cooking; it's processing. I can't emphasize this enough. This means following tested recipes and not improvising, so that the food you process is safe to eat.

Yields are not guaranteed. Like us, Mother Nature has good days and bad ones. A cold, wet spring a few years ago delayed the arrival of strawberries in Washington state, and the lack of sun meant tarter, smaller berries. Taste your raw product before processing so you know what you're dealing with, and be aware that the same volume of produce may yield more or fewer filled jars than the previous year.

Have Fun. In the unlikely event of an unsealed jar, don't fret. Store unsealed goods in the refrigerator and eat within a few weeks.

You're not in this alone. I've curated a list of go-to resources for the ins and outs on the technique and science of preserving, as well as recipes from reliable, trustworthy preservationists (page 217).

Following are some basic recipes; first, here's the general canning procedure. Before you start cooking, get a head start on water bath canning prep and processing:

FROM EMPTY JARS TO FILLED

Prepare the lids. Wash the rings and lids in hot soapy water and rinse well. Set aside.

Sterilize the jars. Use a pot that is deep and wide enough for a canning rack (which holds the jars in place). Make sure the lid is still able to sit on top with the rack inside. Arrange the jars in the canning rack. Add water to the pot until it is at least 1 inch above your jars. *Cover and bring the water to a boil. Keep the jars in the boiling water until ready to process.*

Fill and process. Remove the sterilized jars one by one from the boiling water to a kitchen towel–lined "staging" area. Keep the pot covered and the water boiling. Rest a wide-mouthed funnel on top of a jar and ladle in the pickles or preserves, leaving room at the top, which is called headspace.

With a kitchen towel, wipe clean the rim of the jar. Place the lid on top, then gently screw on the ring (and not too tight). Repeat. Using the jar lifter, return the filled and covered jars to the boiling water. Cover and process according to the recipe.

Cool and store. Transfer the jars to the kitchen towel–lined area and listen for the "ping" of each jar, a sign that you have a proper seal.

Allow to cool for at least 12 hours. Remove the rings. Check once more for a proper seal by lifting each jar by its lid. Label and date the jars and store in a cool, dark place; canned goods keep for up to one year.

BLUEBERRY JAM

- 6 pints blueberries, washed (12 cups)
- 3 to 4 cups granulated sugar
- ¼ cup bottled lemon juice

KITCHEN NOTES: *Six pints of berries are often sold as "half-flats" at farm stands and farmers' markets. Taste the berries for sweetness; if tart, use the higher end of the sugar. If sweet, stick with 3 cups. Use bottled lemon juice rather the juice of fresh lemons; bottled lemon juice has a consistent acid level that conforms with USDA guidelines.*

HERE'S WHAT YOU DO:

Start prepping your jars, as described on page 207.

Place the berries and the sugar in a heavy-bottomed saucepan over medium heat. Stir and bring to a boil, stirring regularly to avoid scalding. Lower the heat and crush the berries with a potato masher until the desired texture is reached. Stir in the lemon juice and cook the mixture until it thickens and gels, adjusting the heat as necessary, about 20 minutes. For those who like a numerical gauge, you're looking for a temperature of 220°F on a candy thermometer. A tip I've picked up from my canning pal Sheri Brooks Vinton, author of *Put 'em Up!*: Let the jam rest for 5 minutes, along with a few stirs, to help release air bubbles.

Following the instructions for filling and processing, rest a wide-mouthed funnel on top of a jar and ladle in the jam, leaving ¼ inch of headspace. Continue to follow the directions on page 207, processing for 10 minutes.

MAKES 8 HALF-PINTS JAM

STRAWBERRY JAM

HERE'S WHAT YOU DO:

Start prepping your jars, as described on page 207. Place the berries and the sugar in a deep, heavy-bottomed saucepan over medium heat. (Strawberries tend to splatter.) Stir and bring to a boil, stirring often to avoid scalding. Lower the heat, stir in the lemon juice, and cook the mixture until it thickens and gels, adjusting the heat as necessary, 20 to 40 minutes, depending on the ripeness of the fruit. The riper the straw-berries, the less natural pectin, thereby requiring more time to gel.

For those who like a numerical gauge, you've got jelled fruit when it reaches 220°F on a candy thermometer. A tip I've picked up from my canning pal Sheri Brooks Vinton, author of *Put 'em Up!*: Once the jam is gelled, let it rest for 5 minutes, along with a few stirs, to help release air bubbles.

Following the instructions for filling and processing, rest a wide-mouthed funnel on top of a jar and ladle in the jam, leaving ¼ inch of headspace. Continue to follow the directions on page 207, processing for 10 minutes.

MAKES ABOUT 8 HALF-PINTS JAM

- 5 pints strawberries, washed and hulled (10 cups)
- 3 to 4 cups granulated sugar
- ¼ cup bottled lemon juice

KITCHEN NOTES: *Six pints of berries are often sold as "half-flats" at farm stands and farmers' markets. Taste the berries for sweetness; if tart, use the higher end of the sugar. If sweet, stick with 3 cups. Use bottled lemon juice rather than the juice of fresh lemons; bottled lemon juice has a consistent acid level that conforms with USDA guidelines. More than any other types of berries, strawberries, when cooked, release a preponderance of foam that rises to the surface. It is perfectly safe (and deli-cious) but may be off putting and looks odd when trapped in a sealed jar. Use a slotted spoon to remove.*

- 2 pounds jalapeño peppers, washed (16 to 20 large or 40 small)
- 1 cup water
- 3 cups distilled white vinegar
- 2 teaspoons kosher salt, or 1¾ teaspoons fine sea salt
- ½ teaspoon ground cumin
- 4 cloves garlic, peeled and left whole

TOOLS: *Disposable gloves*

KITCHEN NOTES: *Most canning books recommend the use of pickling or kosher salt for pickle recipes. As detailed on page 18, I've given up kosher salt for fine sea salt. Keep in mind that the size of salt crystals varies, and as such, so does the volume. As you'll see in the recipe, I recommend about one-fourth less fine sea salt than kosher salt. When shopping, look for salt that says "no additives" on the label—that means the salt is free of anticaking agents, which make for a cloudy (rather than clear) brine and increases the chances of soft (rather than firm) pickles. By all means, use kosher salt if that's what you have on hand; the one thing to avoid for pickling is iodized table salt.*

Please wear disposable gloves when handling chile peppers. The capsaicin found in the seeds and the veins can make life temporarily unpleasant. Wash all work surfaces and tools thoroughly and be careful not to touch your face.

LUCY'S PICKLED JALAPEÑO PEPPERS

I'll admit; I was skeptical when my friend Lucy offered me a taste of her jalapeño pickles sitting atop a tortilla chip. After too many disappointing run-ins with the slimy, chemical-tasting versions on supermarket shelves, I had sworn off them long ago. But her pickles are a revelation—a perfect balance of acid, heat, and garlic—and not the least bit slimy. (Adapted with permission from *Pickled: Preserving a World of Tastes and Traditions* by Lucy Norris.)

HERE'S WHAT YOU DO:

Start prepping your jars, as described on page 207. Put on a pair of disposable gloves. Open a window for ventilation, or if possible, prep the peppers outdoors. Slice the peppers into thin rings, about ¼-inch thick, and transfer to a bowl. Wash your cutting board and knife thoroughly—as well as anything else that may have come in contact with the peppers.

In a nonreactive saucepan (e.g., stainless steel, enameled cast iron, but *not* 100 percent aluminum), whisk together the water, vinegar, salt, and cumin. Bring to a boil over high heat, stirring until the salt dissolves.

Following the directions for filling and processing, pack each sterilized jar tightly with the pepper slices and one whole garlic clove each. Leave enough room at the top so the lid rests easily on the mouth of the jar. Ladle the hot brine to cover the pepper rings leaving ¼ inch of headspace. Continue to follow the directions on page 207, processing for 10 minutes.

Store for about 3 weeks to let the flavors develop before opening. The peppers will turn a dull shade of green. Opened jars can be stored in the fridge for up to 6 months as long as you use clean utensils to take out the pepper rings each time. Sealed, these pickles will keep for about one year.

MAKES 4 PINTS OR 8 HALF-PINTS PICKLES

MAPLE CRANS

HERE'S WHAT YOU DO:

Start prepping your jars, as described on page 207.

Place the cranberries in a medium-size saucepan. Using a zester or grater, remove the zest of two of the oranges, dice, and add to the saucepan. Slice all the oranges in half and squeeze the juice over the cranberries. You want the liquid to barely cover the cranberries; add water as necessary.

Using a liquid measure, add 1½ cups of the maple syrup, reserving the rest on an as-needed basis. Stir the mixture well and bring to a boil.

Lower the heat and cook at a simmer; the cranberries will make a popping noise as they cook, reduce, and thicken. Stir occasionally and cook until desired consistency; taste for the sweet/tart ratio and add more maple syrup as necessary. The cranberries will be ready in as little as 25 minutes.

Following the directions for filling and processing, rest a wide-mouthed funnel on top of a jar and ladle in the cranberries, leaving ¼ inch of headspace. Continue to follow the directions on page 207, processing for 10 minutes.

MAKES 4 HALF-PINTS OF CRANBERRIES

- 2 pounds fresh cranberries, washed thoroughly
- 4 oranges
- 12 to 16 ounces good-quality pure maple syrup, or to taste

KITCHEN NOTES: *This recipe, featured on the Thanksgiving menu, can be made for immediate serving or put up in jars for enjoyment throughout the colder months. I've doubled the amounts for this version to produce four half-pints, which make great winter holiday gifts.*

PRESERVING PARTY

I won't lie; canning is a time-consuming endeavor that requires at least three hours of your undivided attention (and more if you are putting up multiple items). As with any long-haul adventure (see Election Night, page 42), endurance-strength sustenance is an essential component.

I remember one gorgeous August afternoon in 2009 like it was yesterday: A gaggle of my new canning gal pals descended upon my kitchen, where we put up an assortment of Washington state stone fruit: apricots into jam, mustard, and Chinese dipping sauce; and cherries into jam and barbecue sauce. After a few hours, we stepped away from the water bath and sat outside with a family-style salad and some cold rosé. We cackled and told stories and enjoyed the sun on our arms. With our bellies a little fuller and our energy restored, we put the kettle back on and cranked out a few more dozen jars. Everyone went home with an enviable stash and talked about that day for months. Our merry gang has since gotten smaller after the passing of one special lady, also named Kim, so canning on a sunny day in August has new, bittersweet meaning.

THOUGHTS FOR A PRESERVING PARTY (SUMMER)

GREEK-STYLE CHICKPEA PATTIES WITH FETA-YOGURT
    SAUCE ▪ PAGES 140 AND 141

SLICED TOMATOES AND CUCUMBERS

CAESAR-Y ROMAINE SALAD, HOLD THE TOFU CROUTONS ▪ PAGE 162

VANILLA-HONEY FROZEN YOGURT WITH SEASONAL
    FRESH FRUIT ▪ PAGE 202

Action plan: With a little planning, nearly everything on this menu can be done in advance. The day before, assemble the patties, make the Caesar-y dressing, and freeze the yogurt. That morning, wash and dry the romaine lettuce. Fry the patties just before serving, and while they cook, someone can dress the romaine lettuce and slice the tomatoes and cucumbers.

A WEEK OF MENUS AND HOW TO GET A HEAD START ON YOUR WEEK

I've picked a dozen or so dishes from the entire collection that, with some organization and planning on the weekend, can be "dressed down" for Meatless Monday, Tuesday, and so on. A few hours on the weekend cooking up kitchen staples can be time well spent. Following, a week of menus with time-saving tips.

MONDAY

RED BEANS AND (BROWN) RICE

CAJUN BLACKENED TOFU

DO-AHEAD: Make a pot of rice on the weekend and reheat. Dried beans can be soaked and cooked, or use canned beans.

TUESDAY

SOUTHERN-FRIED CHICK . . . PEA PATTIES

CARAMELIZED ONIONS

FINGER-LICKING BARBECUE SAUCE

JICAMA SALAD

DO-AHEAD: Soak the chickpeas the night before, drain in the morning, and keep in the refrigerator until ready to make the patties. Make the sauce and caramelize the onions over the weekend. Both keep well in an airtight container in the refrigerator.

WEDNESDAY

LONG NOODLES WITH SALTED BLACK BEANS
    AND BOK CHOY

DO-AHEAD: Wash and dry the bok choy in the salad spinner earlier in the day. Soak salted black beans while you do the prep for the rest of the dish.

THURSDAY

WOK SALAD OR RAW KALE SALAD

POTATO PIE OR SWEET POTATO–PESTO GRATIN

DO-AHEAD: Wash and dry the romaine or the kale in the salad spinner earlier in the day. Make the pesto over the weekend; it keeps for several days in the refrigerator.

FRIDAY

SPRING FORWARD SOUP

CAESAR-Y ROMAINE SALAD WITH TOFU CROUTONS

DO-AHEAD: Make the soup the previous weekend and freeze. Thaw in the refrigerator in the morning. When ready to cook, first order of business is to drain the tofu. Gently reheat the soup in a saucepan. While the soup is on, make its crostini garnish.

SATURDAY

SOPES WITH BLACK BEANS AND SOFRITO

PINEAPPLE SALSA OR PICO DE GALLO

DO-AHEAD: Make a batch of sofrito over the weekend, pour into a ice cube tray, and freeze. One sofrito cube equals 2 tablespoons. The beans can be soaked and cooked earlier in the week, then flavored with sofrito on the day of cooking.

OR A MEZZE-STYLE COCKTAIL GET-TOGETHER TWO HOURS BEFORE GUESTS ARRIVE

LENTIL PÂTÉ

SWEET POTATO HUMMUS

ROASTED ASPARAGUS WITH GREMOLATA AND
   ALMOND STAR DUST

DO-AHEAD: Roast the sweet potatoes and onions for the hummus while the lentils are simmering for the pâté. Meanwhile, wash and prep the asparagus and pulverize the almonds. While the lentils cool, caramelize the shallots that will season them.

DO-AHEAD DESSERTS

Jam-Dot Cookies: Bake ahead and store in a metal tin, or keep the batter covered in the refrigerator and bake on the fly.

Both the Pumpkin Pudding and Chocolate-Chile Pudding can be made the day before, or in 15 minutes as you need it.

The Molasses Cookie batter can be frozen and used in a slice-and-bake fashion as needed.

A QUART OF ALL-PURPOSE VEG STOCK V GF

In a pinch (which, admittedly is more often than not), I use Rapunzel unsalted vegetable bouillon cubes to make small batches of instant-presto vegetable stock. But because we're talking about getting ahead on meal prep, a batch of all-purpose veg stock is in order. The beauty of homemade stock, as I wrote in *The Meat Lover's Meatless Cookbook* (where this recipe first appeared) is that you can improvise, depending on what you have on hand or what you're in the mood for. Once it's cooled, you can freeze in ice cube trays for the ultimate instant-presto stock.

- 1 leek, thoroughly cleaned, trimmed of its root and cut into fourths (dark green part can be used)
- 1 medium-size onion, cut into quarters, with skin (clean if need be)
- 1 stalk celery, cleaned and cut into thirds
- 3 cloves garlic, peeled but left whole
- 10 black peppercorns
- 5 stripped parsley stems
- 4½ cups cold water
- Add-ons: 1 medium-size carrot, peeled and quartered (optional, for a sweeter result)
- 1 (2 by 1-inch) hunk fresh ginger (optional, for Asian-inspired kapow)
- 1 dried cayenne pepper (optional, for a spicier result)

HERE'S WHAT YOU DO:

Place all the ingredients (including your choice of optional add-ins) in a large saucepan. Bring to a lively simmer, then cook over medium-low heat for 30 minutes. Strain and use as needed. Keeps in the refrigerator for 3 days and in the freezer for several weeks.

METRIC CONVERSIONS

- The recipes in this book have not been tested with metric measurements, so some variations might occur.

- Remember that the weight of dry ingredients varies according to the volume or density factor: 1 cup of flour weighs far less than 1 cup of sugar, and 1 tablespoon doesn't necessarily hold 3 teaspoons.

GENERAL FORMULA FOR METRIC CONVERSION

Ounces to grams	ounces × 28.35 = grams
Grams to ounces	grams × 0.035 = ounces
Pounds to grams	pounds × 453.5 = grams
Pounds to kilograms	pounds × 0.45 = kilograms
Cups to liters	cups × 0.24 = liters
Fahrenheit to Celsius	(°F − 32) × 5 ÷ 9 = °C
Celsius to Fahrenheit	(°C × 9) ÷ 5 + 32 = °F

VOLUME (LIQUID) MEASUREMENTS

1 teaspoon = ⅙ fluid ounce = 5 milliliters

1 tablespoon = ½ fluid ounce = 15 milliliters

2 tablespoons = 1 fluid ounce = 30 milliliters

¼ cup = 2 fluid ounces = 60 milliliters

⅓ cup = 2⅔ fluid ounces = 79 milliliters

½ cup = 4 fluid ounces = 118 milliliters

1 cup or ½ pint = 8 fluid ounces = 250 milliliters

2 cups or 1 pint = 16 fluid ounces = 500 milliliters

4 cups or 1 quart = 32 fluid ounces = 1,000 milliliters

1 gallon = 4 liters

VOLUME (DRY) MEASUREMENTS

¼ teaspoon = 1 milliliter

½ teaspoon = 2 milliliters

¾ teaspoon = 4 milliliters

1 teaspoon = 5 milliliters

1 tablespoon = 15 milliliters

¼ cup = 59 milliliters

⅓ cup = 79 milliliters

½ cup = 118 milliliters

⅔ cup = 158 milliliters

¾ cup = 177 milliliters

1 cup = 225 milliliters

4 cups or 1 quart = 1 liter

½ gallon = 2 liters

1 gallon = 4 liters

OVEN TEMPERATURE EQUIVALENTS, FAHRENHEIT (F) AND CELSIUS (C)

100°F = 38°C

200°F = 95°C

250°F = 120°C

300°F = 150°C

350°F = 180°C

400°F = 205°C

450°F = 230° C

WEIGHT (MASS) MEASUREMENTS

1 ounce = 30 grams

2 ounces = 55 grams

3 ounces = 85 grams

4 ounces = ¼ pound = 125 grams

8 ounces = ½ pound = 240 grams

12 ounces = ¾ pound = 375 grams

16 ounces = 1 pound = 454 grams

LINEAR MEASUREMENTS

½ in = 1½ cm

1 inch = 2½ cm

6 inches = 15 cm

8 inches = 20 cm

10 inches = 25 cm

12 inches = 30 cm

20 inches = 50 cm

RESOURCES

STOCKING THE PANTRY

I'm a proponent of sourcing ingredients and foodstuffs as locally as possible, but I realize that's a tall order for folks in more remote and rural parts of the country. Wherever you live, think beyond the aisles of the big-box store or supermarket; ethnic markets and farmers' markets often stock a wealth of goods and their inventory may surprise you. When I'm running low on a favorite ingredient—and often when I'm not—I refer to this ever-growing go-to list of trusty vendors and suppliers with the goods. On its heels are some of my favorite Web destinations that keep me informed, enlightened, and inspired.

All in Kosher
Online kosher supermarket
http://allinkosher.com

ASIAN GROCERIES

Asiansupermarket365.com
http://asiansupermarket365.com

Asian Market Shopper mobile app by Andrea Nguyen
http://itunes.apple.com/us/app/asian-market-shopper/id436479081?mt=8

BEANS, LEGUMES, GRAINS, NUTS, SEEDS

Bob's Red Mill
Grains, flours, legumes, beans, seeds, plus extensive gluten-free inventory
http://www.bobsredmill.com/

Lundberg Family Farms
Organic and non-GMO brown and white rice, rice flour, and pasta
http://lundberg.com

Massa Organics
Brown rice, almonds
http://www.massaorganics.com/

PNW Co-op Specialty Foods
Washington and Idaho-grown non-GMO lentils, chickpeas, and green split peas
http://www.DavidsonCommodities.com/

Rancho Gordo
Heirloom beans, herbs and spices, and quinoa from the Americas
http://www.ranchogordo.com

CHEESE WRAPPING PAPER

Formaticum
http://www.formaticum.com/

HERBS AND SPICES

World Spice
www.worldspice.com

Penzey's
www.penzeys.com

MEXICAN AND LATIN GROCERIES

www.mexgrocer.com

MIDDLE EASTERN, MEDITERRANEAN, AND SOUTH ASIAN SPECIALTY ITEMS

Kalustyan's
http://kalustyans.com/

OMNIBUS SPECIALTY ITEMS, INCLUDING RICE BRAN OIL

Chef Shop
http://chefshop.com/

RICE BRAN OIL

California Rice Oil
http://www.californiariceoil.com/

SALT

The Meadow
www.atthemeadow.com/shop/

SPANISH AND MEDITERRANEAN GROCERIES AND KITCHEN ITEMS

La Tienda
www.latienda.com

FEEDING YOUR BRAIN

Art of the Pie
Pie philosophy and instruction from teacher Kate McDermott
http://artofthepie.com

Canning Across America
A collective dedicated to the revival of the lost art of putting up food, which I cofounded in 2009
http://www.canningacrossamerica.com

The Cook's Thesaurus
http://www.foodsubs.com/

Ecocentric: A blog about food, water and energy
http://www.ecocentricblog.org/

Environmental Working Group's Shopper's Guide to Pesticides in Produce
http://www.ewg.org/foodnews/summary/

Farmers' markets list from the USDA
http://search.ams.usda.gov/farmersmarkets/

Food in Jars
The lively and informative blog of avid preserver and author Marisa McClellan
http://foodinjars.com

Food Safety News
http://www.foodsafetynews.com/

Meatless Monday
www.meatlessmonday.com

National Center for Home Food Preservation
http://nchfp.uga.edu

Non-GMO Project
http://www.nongmoproject.org

Non-GMO Shoppers Guide, from the Center for Food Safety
http://truefoodnow.org/shoppers-guide/

The Oldways Vegetarian Diet Pyramid
http://www.oldwayspt.org/vegetarian-diet-pyramid

Seasonal Produce Map by Month from Epicurious
http://www.epicurious.com/articles/guides/seasonalcooking/farmtotable/seasonalingredientmap

Vegetarian Resource Group
http://vrg.org

Whole Grains A to Z Explainer by the Whole Grains Council
http://www.wholegrainscouncil.org/whole-grains-101/whole-grains-a-to-z

The World's Healthiest Foods
http://whfoods.com/

Finding KOD
www.kimodonnel.com

GRATITUDE

A lot of people breathed life into this project, a collective act of kindness and good will for which I am deeply grateful.

A big shout-out to the trusty and insightful crew of volunteer recipe testers, many who've been on board since *The Meat Lover's Meatless Cookbook*:

Ben Abramson, Jason Bazilian and Wendy Bazilian, David Bennett, Gillian Bonazoli, Lise Bradford, Jules Cechony, Jacqueline Church, Dennis Coyle, Traci Darnell, Lisa Davis, Margit Detweiler, Susan Detweiler, Jim Eber, Sally Ekus, Corinne Fay, Stefanie Gans, Erin Hare, Leslie Hatfield and John Connolly, Melanie Haupt, Leslie Kelly, Liz Kelly-Nelson and Dot Kelly, Susan Mack, Cynthia Morrell, Susan O'Donnel, Joyce Pinson, Natalie Rahn, Clodagh Reeves, Christopher Rowe and Gwenda Bond, Steven Shapiro, Jen Sieve-Hicks, Brook Stephens, Mitchell Story, Stacey Stern, Marjory Sweet, Kerry Trueman and Matt Rosenberg, Elizabeth Terry, Jennifer Young.

An extra squeeze to David Bennett, Susan Mack, and Jen Sieve-Hicks who went above and beyond the call to test whatever I sent their way, early and often.

To Stephanie Gailing, Jeanne Sauvage, and Leslie Silverman for reading and rereading, advising and cheerleading, ever-steadfast and supportive, any time of day or night, thank you thank you.

To Jim Eber, who's been there since before the first book was even a seedling, who can talk both business and bean burgers, always rooting for me and yet never too shy to dish out the tough love when I need a kick in the pants.

To my agents Lisa Ekus and Sally Ekus, who have become like family, courage and kindness incarnate, grace and integrity always.

To Renée Sedliar, who continues to be my editing shepherd, not just in title but by example and in spirit.

To Kate McDermott, who tirelessly spent the better part of three months with me developing and testing the pie dough recipe featured in these pages. Her passion for pie and how it's a metaphor for life has rubbed off on me and the ink is indelible.

Un beso por cookbook author Sandra A. Gutierrez, who graciously shared her knowledge, time, and recipe for *sopes*.

To pickle princess and canning sister Lucy Norris, who generously shared her recipe for pickled jalapeños, which everyone and their mother should make.

To cookbook authors and scholars Monica Bhide, Maria Speck, and Grace Young for sharing their wisdom and insight.

To photographer Clare Barboza, whose beautiful images you see on these pages, and whose eye will take her far in life.

To Brook Stephens, who cooked, cleaned, tested, tasted, and never complained, a trouper of troupers who's become a dear friend and cook-sister.

To Kim Davidson at PNW Co-op Specialty Foods, for her generous donation of sustainably grown non-GMO legumes during several months of recipe development and testing.

As I did with *The Meat Lover's Meatless Cookbook*, I spent several weeks holed up in Eureka Springs, Arkansas, at the Writer's Colony at Dairy Hollow, where I always meet the muse. My community in this hard-to-describe hamlet has become a second family: Catherina Bernstein, Mary Pat Boian, Vicki Kell-Schneider, Barbara Kennedy, Karen Lindblad, Sandy Martin, Amanda and Robb Shoeman, Virginia Voiers, David "Fuzzy" White, and the merry crew at the Eureka Farmers' Market.

To my dear sweet Russell, who's my champion, my person, and the reason I feel hopeful about the world. You are a beacon of kindness. My love for you is in the corners, crevices, and sidewalk cracks.

In memory of my father, John, and my father-in-law, Hughes, and to two bright stars that shone over Seattle, Kim Ricketts and Christina Choi.

INDEX